Building Executive Fu...

Educators clamor to provide top-notch lessons and resources for students, but if students lack executive function, even the best materials won't produce the desired results. If students haven't developed the brain-based skills to focus, catch and correct errors, identify cause-and-effect relationships, and more, they can't make sense of lessons. Executive function is the missing link to student achievement. But how can you develop this in the classroom?

In this new book, bestselling author Nancy Sulla has the answers. She explains how building executive function requires a combination of activities, structures, and teacher facilitation strategies aimed at six increasingly complex life skills that should be the goal of any school: conscious control, engagement, collaboration, empowerment, efficacy, and leadership. She also offers a variety of examples, activities, and structures fit for every grade level and subject area. With the book's practical strategies and tools, you will be inspired, armed, and ready to establish a clear framework for building executive function in all your students.

Nancy Sulla is the founder and President of IDE Corp. (Innovative Designs for Education), a consulting company specializing in instructional and organizational design.

Also Available from Nancy Sulla
(www.routledge.com/eyeoneducation)

It's Not What You Teach but How:
7 Insights to Making the CCSS Work for You

Students Taking Charge in Grades 6–12:
Inside the Learner-Active, Technology-Infused Classroom

Students Taking Charge in Grades K–5:
Inside the Learner-Active, Technology-Infused Classroom

Students Taking Charge:
Implementation Guide for Leaders
With Tanya Bosco and Julie Marks

Building Executive Function

The Missing Link to Student Achievement

Nancy Sulla

Routledge
Taylor & Francis Group

NEW YORK AND LONDON

First published 2018
by Routledge
711 Third Avenue, New York, NY 10017

and by Routledge
2 Park Square, Milton Park, Abingdon, Oxon, OX14 4RN

Routledge is an imprint of the Taylor & Francis Group, an informa business

Library of Congress Cataloging in Publication Data
Names: Sulla, Nancy, author.
Title: Building executive function: the missing link to
student achievement / by Nancy Sulla.
Description: New York: Routledge, 2017. |
Includes bibliographical references.
Identifiers: LCCN 2017020366 | ISBN 9781138632028 (hbk) |
ISBN 9781138632035 (pbk) | ISBN 9781315208497 (ebk)
Subjects: LCSH: Cognitive learning. | Executive functions
(Neuropsychology) | Academic achievement–Psychological aspects.
Classification: LCC LB1062 .S825 2017 | DDC 370.15–dc23
LC record available at https://lccn.loc.gov/2017020366

ISBN: 978-1-138-63202-8 (hbk)
ISBN: 978-1-138-63203-5 (pbk)
ISBN: 978-1-315-20849-7 (ebk)

Typeset in Palatino
by Deanta Global Publishing Services, Chennai, India

Visit the eResources: www.routledge.com/9781138632035

To my sister Marge, gone too soon, who worked as a school psychologist with disadvantaged children in Appalachia, building executive function skills before we knew it was fashionable. We're still at it, Marge!

Meet the Author

Nancy Sulla is the creator of the *Learner-Active, Technology-Infused Classroom*—a student-driven classroom framework that puts students in charge of their own learning. She is the founder and President of IDE Corp. (Innovative Designs for Education), an educational consulting company specializing in transformational professional development. She holds a B.A. in Education from Fairleigh Dickinson University, an M.A. in Computer Science from Montclair University, and an Ed.D. in Educational Administration from Fordham University. Her diverse background includes teaching at the elementary, middle school, high school, and college levels; working as a computer programmer and systems analyst; and leading teachers as a district administrator prior to launching IDE Corp.

Nancy's passion for changing the world through redesigning the culture and pedagogy of school fuels her writing and consulting. She focuses on helping schools design problem-based, student-driven, *Learner-Active, Technology-Infused Classrooms*; designing experiential schools that address the interests and needs of all students; and taking a systems approach to educational leadership.

Contents

eResources

The tools in the Appendix of this book will also be available as free eResources ⬇, so you can easily download and print them for classroom use.

You can access them by visiting the book product page: www.routledge.com/9781138632035. Click on the tab that says "eResources" and select the files. They will begin downloading to your computer.

Acknowledgments

I am most grateful to the many educators who are changing the world through their amazing *Learner-Active, Technology-Infused Classrooms*. I wish I could name you all! I have such respect for you for stepping outside your comfort zones to challenge your belief systems and shift paradigms: to go from being ferries to bridge builders. I am humbled in your presence. I must give a shout out to Chester W. Taylor Elementary School principal Julie Marks and the first group of kindergarten and fourth-grade teachers to launch their *Learner-Active, Technology-Infused Classrooms* there. You were the inspiration for this book, as you will read in the introduction.

As always, my collaboration with my talented, dedicated, and gritty colleagues at IDE Corp. fuels my daily work. You guys rock! Thanks for the feedback, stories, midnight email responses, and support while I wrote this book. Lauren Davis, my publisher, you continue to come to my rescue when my mind is blocked and inspire me with your unwavering belief in my work.

I am drawn to the spirit of the woman who was the first to map the prefrontal cortex in the seventies and open the door to further study of executive function, Patricia Goldman-Rakic. While she is no longer walking this Earth, her words and work mesmerize me.

With the advent of Twitter, I am further supported by a wonderful PLN of educators with whom I've had the pleasure of countless hours of sharing and inspiration, including, most notably, #leadupchat, #satchatwc, #engagechat, #dtk12chat, and our own group, #LATICchat.

Introduction

When my sister and I were young and would misbehave, rarely of course, my father would sit us down to discuss our actions and the consequences of those actions. I remember we used to say, "Just punish us!" We loathed the lengthy discussions of our wrong-doings. Our friends were either punished or grounded, but not us; we were engaged in discussion. I look back and think of how my father was a natural at teaching us *cause-and-effect, seeing multiple sides to a situation, considering future consequences in light of current action*, and more of what I now know to be the skills of executive function.

I designed my student-driven *Learner-Active, Technology-Infused Classroom* (#LATIC) model in the seventies when I was teaching. It later became the cornerstone of my consulting career and my company, IDE Corp. My intent was to combat student boredom with school and put students in charge of their own learning, building student responsibility, engagement, and academic rigor. Over the years, I realized that something else was happening in those classrooms that propelled student learning. It wasn't that I was teaching teachers how to present a better lesson; it had to be something related to students taking charge of their own learning. It was when we expanded our work to Florida, in working with principal Julie Marks and the kindergarten and fourth- grade teachers at Chester W. Taylor Elementary School, that the pieces started to fall into place. These teachers were involved in the first-year rollout of designing a *Learner-Active, Technology-Infused School*. The teachers so enthusiastically worked as two well-oiled teams in designing their classrooms; they were "all in" as grade levels. The principal set her expectations for implementing my model and supported the teachers throughout, spending considerable time in classrooms, inspiring and assisting teachers in implementing the *Learner-Active, Technology-Infused Classroom* with fidelity. The students the school serves come from economically disadvantaged homes and struggle academically, so the gains were clearly visible. In thinking through the success stories over the decades of my work, I suddenly realized that the "missing link" that was being addressed by the model was executive function. The structures of the *Learner-Active, Technology-Infused Classroom* seemed to organically support the growth of executive function. Needless to say, I had to research the topic further, and then came this book! All the teachers in the school, grade level and special area, now run *Learner-Active, Technology-Infused Classrooms*, making them the first fully #LATIC school in Florida.

You don't need to be running a *Learner-Active, Technology-Infused Classroom* to use the strategies in this book to build executive function. If you are, however, I've noted all the #LATIC structures referenced by capitalizing them. The executive function skills in the book are italicized. And you'll see, too, a set of Twitter hashtags for the various aspects of executive function. This book will come alive if all who are reading it start tweeting out their stories, pics, structures, and thoughts about executive function; so, tweet away!

I hope the book will help you to think more deliberately about all the structures, activities, and facilitation strategies you can use to develop executive function in your students. The more you think through the deliberate activation of executive function, the more it will just become a part of the way you think about teaching and learning.

I do have my policy hopes with this book as well. While the overemphasis on ELA and math instruction to address state tests appears, on the surface, to make sense, the reality is that students engage considerably in the types of activities and thinking that build executive function while engaging in the arts, physical education, social studies, and science. That means that studying the arts could improve a student's math score! As a fourth-grade teacher, I inspired all my students to sign up for chorus and instrumental music lessons. As a middle school math teacher, I took my class outside regularly to study math by playing kickball. The marginalizing of some of these content areas and reduction in time spent engaged in them is, I believe, doing a disservice to our students and hindering their overall achievement. We need to look at learning as an interrelated system of studies, with all content areas supporting one another: the connecting thread being executive function.

Throughout the book you will see specific Twitter hashtags related to building executive function: #EF_ConsciousControl; #EF_Engagement; #EF_Collaboration; #EF_Empowerment; #EF_Efficacy; and #EF_Leadership. I hope you'll use these to post your successes, resources you develop, classroom pictures, and questions to broaden the educational conversation on the importance of executive function for all.

The Power, Promise, and Pitfalls of Executive Function

See if you can envision this. You have a 2" nail hammered partway into a piece of wood; your goal is to drive the nail all the way in. Have you got the picture? You start applying pressure with the palm of your hand; but no matter how hard or long you push, the nail does not move. You then step back from the situation and get a hammer. With a few quick strokes of the hammer, the nail moves through the wood to its destination.

You have students who attend class and have some background content but need to master a lot more to achieve at the desired level. You start teaching lessons and purchasing materials that break down the content into seemingly reasonable steps for one to learn. But your students aren't achieving at the desired level. You then take a step back and shift your focus to building executive function, and students begin achieving at higher levels of content mastery.

Do you see the metaphor here? Do you understand it? If so, you've just demonstrated your strength in executive function. Were you able to *create a mental image* of the nail-into-board scenario? Were you able to *hold on to information while considering other information* when you read the second paragraph after reading the first? Were you able to consider the *cause-and-effect relationships* of hitting the nail with the palm of a hand versus hitting it with the hammer? Were you able to *shift focus from one event to another* when you ended the hammer-and-nail paragraph and read the executive function and achievement paragraph? Were you able to *think about multiple concepts simultaneously* after reading both and engaging in a comparison? Were you able to *focus* and *concentrate* while reading those two paragraphs? Having those italicized skills made the text accessible to you. If you did not have those skills, you could have read those paragraphs over and over again, to no avail. Trying harder wouldn't have gotten you further down the road of understanding. These are just some of the skills of executive function: a set of skills that help direct the management of information and behavior.

Now consider a possible home scenario. You open a door, pushing it a little too hard; it slams into the wall behind it, punching a hole in the drywall. You think, "I bet I can learn how to fix this and save the expense of hiring someone." Where will you find out how to accomplish this task? With a quick Web search, you find a how-to sheet of directions with text and pictures; you also find a video of someone demonstrating and explaining the process. Easy! Well, not so fast. Review the list of executive function skills in Table 1.1 and check off the ones you will need in order to process this information you found, that is, to successfully follow the video or direction sheet and patch the hole.

I checked off about two dozen skills without which the hole will not be patched. You can have a direction sheet on how to spackle a wall, but if you can't *shift focus from one event* (reading the directions) *to another* (spackling the wall), those directions will be useless. If you can't *persist in a task*, you'll soon find a jar of spackle and a spackling knife sitting on the floor while you're off engaging in some other activity, and the hole in the wall remains.

Table 1.1

❏ Attending to a person or activity	❏ Thinking about multiple concepts simultaneously
❏ Focusing	❏ Setting goals
❏ Concentrating	❏ Managing time
❏ Thinking before acting	❏ Working towards a goal
❏ Initiating a task	❏ Organizing actions and thoughts
❏ Persisting in a task	❏ Considering future consequences in light of current action
❏ Maintaining social appropriateness	
❏ Storing and manipulating visual and verbal information	❏ Making hypotheses, deductions, and inferences
❏ Identifying same and different	❏ Applying former approaches to new situations
❏ Remembering details	❏ Defining a problem
❏ Following multiple steps	❏ Analyzing
❏ Holding on to information while considering other information	❏ Creating mental images
	❏ Generating possible solutions
❏ Identifying cause-and-effect relationships	❏ Anticipating
	❏ Predicting outcomes
❏ Categorizing information	❏ Evaluating
❏ Shifting focus from one event to another	❏ Self-assessing
❏ Changing perspective	❏ Overcoming temptation
❏ Seeing multiple sides of a situation	❏ Monitoring performance
❏ Being open to others' points of view	❏ Reflecting on goals
❏ Being creative	❏ Managing conflicting thoughts
❏ Catching and correcting errors	

Consider that today, with increased access to the Internet and more people uploading professional and amateur "how to" videos and direction sheets, you can locate information on nearly any topic you wish to pursue. If you search for "subtraction with regrouping," you'll find a wealth of resources. If you search for "light and shade in oil painting," "basketball jump shot," "how to use a gluestick," or "balancing chemical equations," you'll likewise have no lack of resources. Many of the skills and concepts students need to learn are readily available through a variety of sources on the Internet. This is far different from the accessibility to content that was available just a decade ago. What *is* important, however, is that you can identify a *reliable* source, and that requires executive function. Likewise, being able to take in the content information and translate that into learning requires executive function. So, with all the "physical access" students may have to the Internet in school and at home, only the possession of strong executive function skills will provide them with the "cognitive access" to the content that will lead to learning. Physical access to content through lessons does not equal the cognitive access that leads to learning. Without the skills of executive function, you cannot access the information needed to transform thinking and produce powerful learning. Executive function is, therefore, the coveted missing link to student achievement.

Schools seeking to improve student achievement tend to invest in textbooks, computer programs, curricular programs, and related professional development on teaching lesson-level content. While an effective lesson and great materials may be necessary to learning, they are not sufficient to ensure learning. They will be to little or no avail with a student who lacks executive function. The key to unlocking content and ensuring a pathway to long-term memory is through executive function.

What is Executive Function?

"The executive functions are a set of processes that all have to do with managing oneself and one's resources in order to achieve a goal. [Executive function] is an umbrella term for the neurologically based skills involving mental control and self-regulation" (Cooper-Kahn, Dietzel, 2008, p. 10). While there is no one universally accepted definition of the term *executive function*, this one reflects most other definitions.

What is intriguing is the connection between the definition of executive function and the prefrontal cortex: the part of the brain most involved in the development of these skills. Early definitions of executive function from the 1970s refer to those skills that are handled by the prefrontal cortex, while the prefrontal cortex has been defined as the part of the brain that handles execu-

Table 1.2   Executive Function Skills

Organization
   Working Memory
   Cognitive Flexibility
   Planning
   Reasoning
   Problem-Solving
Self-Regulation
   Inhibitory Control
   Self-Awareness

---

tive function. The prefrontal cortex develops skills of executive function, while developing those skills further develops the prefrontal cortex. That is because the prefrontal cortex continues significant development after birth into adolescence and is not fully matured until the mid-twenties. Thus, the "I use; I grow" relationship is characteristic of executive function and the prefrontal cortex.

Russell Barkley (2012) explores the various definitions of executive function and provides his own synthesis: "The use of self-directed actions so as to choose goals and to select, enact, and sustain actions across time toward those goals usually in the context of others often relying on social and cultural means for the maximization of one's long-term welfare as the person defines that to be" (p. 171). The prominent concept in the various definitions is that we choose to use executive function skills to advance our goals. If I want a treat, I may have to *overcome temptation* to misbehave; if I want to solve the puzzle, I may have to *create mental images*, *anticipate*, and *evaluate* my actions; if I want to finish my chores so I can go and play, I may have to *set goals*, *manage time*, and *persist in a task*; and so forth. The skills, as I present them here, fall into two overarching categories: organization and self-regulation (see Table 1.2). Each of these subcategories contains a set of more specific executive function skills (see Appendix A).

While you may find varied lists of skills compiled by others, they all tend to focus on these overarching categories and skills. And the list of skills outlined in Appendix A can serve as a great resource for you as you rethink classroom instruction and the teaching – learning relationship.

Redefining "The Basics" of Curricular Content

Have you ever attempted to teach a student new content and presented what you felt was a very good lesson, demonstration, or explanation, only to find yourself frustrated that the student wasn't able to follow along and understand the content? Teachers learn to begin lessons by activating prior knowledge. A lesson on adjectives, for example, typically begins with a recall of nouns and their purpose and then moves to brainstorming words that describe nouns. Schools tend to define "the basics" of a subject area in terms of skills and concepts within that subject area, but it may be that the path to achievement runs deeper than that. Perhaps the basics of understanding adjectives, for example, aren't simply understanding nouns and the concept of description. *Thinking about multiple concepts simultaneously, categorizing information, identifying same and different, storing and manipulating visual and verbal information, persisting in a task*, and other skills should be considered the true foundations for understanding adjectives. Without those skills, no matter what a teacher presents, students will fall short of achieving an understanding of adjectives. I'm not suggesting that teachers eliminate content instruction; I'm suggesting teachers create a foundation of executive function such that students can cognitively access that content (see Table 1.3).

The foundational skills for learning to recite the alphabet include *attending to a task, focusing, storing verbal information*, and *persisting in a task*. The foundational skills for understanding the causes and outcomes of World War II include *identifying cause-and-effect relationships, seeing multiple sides of a situation, considering future consequences in light of current action*, and *analyzing*, to name a few. The foundational skills for performing a piece of music include *concentrating, working towards a goal, monitoring performance, evaluating, catching and correcting errors*, and *persisting in a task*. The foundational skills for writing a fictional story include *creating mental images; being creative; organizing thoughts; making hypotheses, deductions, and inferences;* and *remembering details*. Discussing an experiment includes the foundational skills of *attending to a person or activity, concentration, shifting focus from one event to another, maintaining social appropriateness, seeing multiple sides to a situation, managing conflicting thoughts*, and *overcoming temptation*. The foundational skills of sketching a still life of apples might be *shifting focus from one event to another, analyzing, changing perspective, organizing actions and thoughts, monitoring performance*, and *applying former approaches to new situations*.

Table 1.3 To Master the Concept of the Adjective

You Need To	*Which Means You Can*	*Which Means You Can*
• Think about multiple concepts simultaneously • Categorize information • Identify same and different • Store and manipulate verbal and visual information • Persist in a task	• Understand and use words • Understand and use nouns • Understand the concept of description • Describe people, places, and things	• Understand and use adjectives

Cognitive Access

Given that more traditional "lessons" that were once the monopoly of teachers are now readily available through other venues, such as the Internet, the role of the teacher and the focus of school instruction must shift. Students who possess strong executive function skills can cognitively access a lesson and learn from it; those who do not possess strong executive function cannot.

The same is true for a classroom teacher's lesson. Those students who possess strong executive function can pay attention, follow along, and construct meaning from the information. Those who do not possess strong executive function will learn little, regardless of how accomplished and talented the teacher is. The achievement gaps that exist in schools today, therefore, may be more a matter of the brain's (cognitive) accessibility to content—that is, through executive function skills—than access to instruction.

While the spotlight on executive function first appeared in the world of special education, the reality is that growth in executive function skills is needed by all students. Many students in regular education classrooms who are not identified for services related to special education struggle with academic achievement. The part of the brain that controls executive function does not fully develop naturally until the age of 25; thus, anyone under that age who is challenged in the area of achievement may benefit from a focus on executive function. If you've ever heard anyone, including yourself, address a teenager or young adult with the question, "What were you thinking?" you can be sure that executive function was at the core of that frustration.

The value of teachers, therefore, goes far beyond presenting content presentation. If schools can help enhance and advance brain development related to executive function, they can provide their students with much greater cognitive accessibility to learning and higher-order reasoning and protect them from the many unhealthy decisions that they might otherwise make. With executive function as the missing link to student achievement, schools cannot afford to let it be a topic of conversation only in special education circles; executive function must dominate the conversation of educational pedagogy.

Preparing Students for Their Future

As of the writing of this book, the world had just entered what is known as the Fourth Industrial Revolution (World Economic Forum, 2016). The First Industrial Revolution was ushered in by the invention of the steam engine; the Second was characterized by the use of electricity for mass production and the rise of the factory; and the Third had as its hallmark computer technology and automation. Computers can automate many jobs for greater speed, accuracy, and efficiency. This caused a shift in the workforce towards humans moving off the production line and, instead, handling jobs that require design, personalization, and service. With the Fourth Industrial Revolution and the rise of artificial intelligence, the computer no longer has to depend on its programmer to offer it new capabilities. Systems of computers interacting with one another, the environment, and humans are poised to design their own future systems, making them less dependent upon programmers. They have the ability to be adaptive, robust, predictive, and anticipatory.

"The Future of Jobs" report (World Economic Forum, 2016) offers some insight into the near future. An estimated 65% of students entering kindergarten today will graduate and work in jobs that don't exist today. In-demand skills are shifting from the technical to the social: "persuasion, emotional intelligence and teaching others" (WEF, 2016, p. 3). While technical skills will continue to be important, they must be coupled with strong social skills and the ability to collaborate. Data-analysis and presentation skills will be in demand across job sectors. Such higher-order skills are the realm of the prefrontal cortex and executive function. These insights point to the need to help students maximize their executive function abilities to learn at levels beyond simple content acquisition. Let's begin with the origin of executive function: the prefrontal cortex of the brain.

What's in a Brain?

To understand executive function, it is helpful to become familiar with the physiology and development of the human brain. The brain is composed of specialized cells called neurons, referred to informally as "gray matter" (Figure 1.1).

Neurons have all these little projections off them called *dendrites*. The dendrites are the message receivers. Neurons also each have one long axon, which projects out from the neuron and ends with another cluster of axon terminals. That long axon is referred to as "white matter": more on that a little later.

The neuron sends out signals in the form of chemicals that travel down the axon to the axon terminals, which are positioned close to the dendrites of another neuron. The tiny space between the axon terminal of one neuron and the dendrite of another is known as a synapse. The chemical is fired from the axon of one neuron, across the synapse, to the dendrite of another neuron. The more signals that are fired between two neurons, the stronger the connection, thus building brainpower, if you will. To put these neurons

Figure 1.1

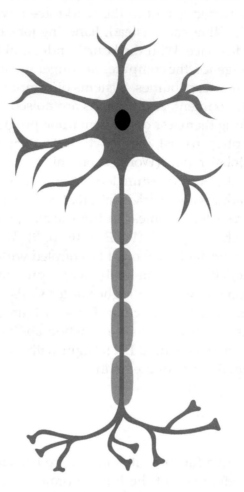

in perspective, the average human adult brain has approximately 100 billion neurons, each of which is connected to up to 10,000 other neurons. That's one quadrillion connections being managed by the brain!

As educators, we often refer to a student's prior knowledge, or *schema*. This means that an existing, strong neural network is holding information for the student to retrieve and use. As young children enter school, their brains, and particularly the prefrontal cortex, are undergoing what is known as a synaptic proliferation: Many new synapses are becoming strengthened, representing learning. The more experiences, the more practice, the more engagement with content, the more synapses will become strengthened and, therefore, the more gray matter is being created. This is why it is so important that our younger learners' days are filled with varied experiences and hands-on exploration.

As the brain matures, the axons become covered with a myelin sheath to protect them, a process known as myelination. This increases the speed of the signals flowing down the axon, thus improving the brain's memory and processing speed. The axon and its myelin sheath represent the white matter in the brain.

Typical Brain Development for Executive Function

The brain is typically described as being made up of various regions, each of which handles different functions, from breathing and movement to emotions and complex thought. At the front of the brain, just behind the forehead, is the prefrontal cortex, which handles most executive function skills. From birth, the prefrontal cortex continues to develop steadily, with inhibitory control and working memory being the first executive functions to solidify. The dendrites and connections in the prefrontal cortex grow by use. The more students hear language, the greater their ability; the more they see objects and hear objects' names, the more able they are to learn names of objects. Thus, the more executive function skills students encounter, the more the prefrontal cortex grows. The more you ask a young child to identify same and different, follow multiple steps, categorize, and be creative, the more the prefrontal cortex that handles these executive function skills grows.

The brain then undergoes significant growth between the ages of four and five, which you'll note if you work with or have been around four and five-year-olds. For four-year-olds, the reality that they can't do or have what they want feels like the end of the world. Then, within a year, five-year-olds with typical brain development seem to have a much more reasonable view of reality. They can delay gratification, understand simple cause-and-effect relationships, *consider future consequences in light of current action*, and so forth.

Stanford's Marshmallow Test

You may have heard of Stanford University's "Marshmallow Test," which is described in more detail in Walter Mischel's book *The Marshmallow Test: Mastering Self-Control* (2014). Mischel, a researcher at Stanford, conducted an experiment in the 1960s and 1970s with over 600 children between the ages of four and six to study the ability of a child to delay gratification. The child was placed in a room, seated at a table. The test administrator placed one large marshmallow in front of the child and said that the child could eat the marshmallow now or wait for the test administrator's return with a second marshmallow, at which time the child could eat both. The test administrator then waited approximately 15 minutes before returning with the second marshmallow. A minority of the children ate the first marshmallow immediately. Most attempted to wait, using self-talk and distracting themselves from the marshmallow. Approximately a third actually waited the full time and received the reward. Age was a major determinant in the child's ability to delay gratification, further supporting the belief that executive function skills increase with the growth of the prefrontal cortex between the ages of four and six. Experience in the skills listed in Appendix A will be key to prefrontal cortex growth in primary and elementary students.

Adolescence

During adolescence, the prefrontal cortex undergoes a second substantial growth phase, known as *synaptic proliferation*, and a pruning phase. Those synapses that are not regularly used are pruned and are no longer available for use by the neuron. This relates to the "use it or lose it" phrase: If a youngster is learning piano and practicing regularly, most likely the brain's neurons will be firing and solidifying the connections and, thus, the capability. If a youngster has a few piano lessons and then stops playing, those unused synapses will eventually atrophy and the learning will most likely be lost.

The pruning process combined with myelination actually make the brain more effective and the prefrontal cortex stronger. However, during the pruning process, which typically occurs at puberty, the brain loses gray matter. Additionally, the brain matures from back to front, meaning that the prefrontal cortex is the last to mature, around the age of 25. Meanwhile, the part of the brain that reacts to pleasure and rewards is located at the back of the brain and therefore matures during adolescence, while the prefrontal cortex, which handles reasoning and judgment, is still developing. Adolescents are particularly prone to whatever stimulates the pleasure sensors of the brain, yet they have little ability to effectively evaluate those and make healthy judgments. Add hormones to that mix and you have the typical teenager! Teenagers need cues and protocols for surviving those teenage years. Once the growth spurt of pruning and myelination processes starts slowing down, a teenager has one powerful brain!

The Effect of Stress on the Prefrontal Cortex

Stress is not good for anyone's overall health, but it is particularly harmful for the developing prefrontal cortex. Children who live under chronic stress, which could include poverty, domestic violence, emotionally or physically abusive parents, protracted divorce, and so on, tend to demonstrate lower levels of executive function. It is important to understand the impact of stress on the body.

Built into the human body, from the beginning of our days on Earth, is a "flight or fight" response to danger. If you are being attacked by a wild animal, for example, you have two choices: attempt to fight it, or run as fast as you can. Deep inside the brain is an almond-shaped area known as the hypothalamus; it exists in all vertebrate animals. Its job is to make a connection between your central nervous system (brain, spinal cord) and the endocrine system, whose job it is to send hormones to targeted organs based on the body's need. At the first sign of a stressful situation, your hypothalamus sends a signal to the pituitary gland (a pea-sized gland just below the hypothalamus), which sends a signal to the adrenal glands that sit atop the kidneys. One of the functions of the adrenal glands is to secrete adrenaline and cortisol in the face of stress. Adrenaline immediately focuses your attention on the problem and provides you with that rush of energy. You've most likely experienced it when you were in a near accident: having an animal run out in front of you while driving and having to steer clear of an accident, jumping out of the way of a falling object, and so on. You feel that rush, your heart starts pounding faster, you seem to visualize in slow motion so you can focus, and you may sweat. That's adrenaline, the first responder to stress, which is putting your body in motion. It dissipates as quickly as it is created, so your body does not build up adrenaline during stress.

Immediately following adrenaline is cortisol, which pumps glucose into the large muscles that are in your legs and arms, thus enabling you to fight or flee. The body draws energy away from the less important functions when you're fighting or fleeing in a stressful situation. Those include digestion and the development of the prefrontal cortex. Consider that when you're dealing with an animal attack, you really don't need to digest that meal, nor do you need to focus on higher-order reasoning. The body cannot distinguish between the stress of a charging animal and seeing your mom break down because she can't pay the bills, or being told you have to pack your things and leave your home, or being the victim or viewer of abuse. In these situations, you don't need to fight or flee, so all that glucose entering your system goes unused, building up in the body.

Young children who live in significantly stressful situations experience chronically high levels of cortisol in their systems. Chronic levels of cortisol lead to dendritic atrophy—big words that mean that those dendrites that are firing chemicals across synapses to build brain capacity are shriveling up. The brains of "stressed-out" children are literally less physiologically capable of learning than they would be without stress.

Hope for Advancing the Growth of the Prefrontal Cortex

Phineas Gage was a railroad construction foreman in 1848. In blasting through rock, the workers would pack dynamite into blasting holes, using a long tamping iron, and then ignite it. Somehow, Gage was distracted in the process and the dynamite ignited while the tamping iron was still in the hole. It shot out of the hole, thrust upward through the explosion, pierced Gage's jaw, destroyed a molar, took out his eye, and exited at the middle front of his skull, just below his hairline. After the accident, Gage was conscious and sat upright while transported by horse and carriage back to his house. He spoke with Dr. John Harlowe throughout the immediate treatment. The rod had sliced through Gage's prefrontal cortex, but it did not seemingly affect any life-supporting areas of the brain. Gage was 25 years old at the time. Three key events paved the way for what we know today about executive function and the prefrontal cortex.

First, Gage's doctor and friends found that, after the accident, his personality had changed considerably, to the point where his friends referred to him as "no longer Gage." His doctor's notes indicated that Gage had outbursts of profanities, could not stick to plans, cared little for others, and was impulsive. Gage had survived the accident with no damage to his motor skills or basic brain functions; the rod had only destroyed a section of his prefrontal cortex, an area not closely related to human survival. However, his doctor was intrigued by the effects of the destruction of that part of the brain. His executive function skills, as we define them today (see Appendix A), were greatly impaired.

The second event came years later, when Dr. Harlowe tracked down the family after Gage's death only to find that he had resumed a fairly normal life, even holding a job as a stagecoach driver in Chile before returning to San Francisco where he died of a seizure, believed to be related to the accident, at age 37. At the doctor's request, Gage's body was exhumed and the skull and tamping iron were given to the doctor. They reside today at a museum at Harvard Medical School.

Thirdly, in the 1970s, a psychologist and historian by the name of Malcolm Macmillan took an interest in the story of Phineas Gage. For more than 40 years, he has studied the accounts of the accident. One day, Macmillan was watching Queen Elizabeth's husband, Prince Philip, racing horse coaches, and he realized that they were similar to those that Gage would have ridden in Chile. As he watched the intricate movements that Prince Philip made to the reins, he realized that Gage could not possibly have performed those functions without executive function, and thus, an intact prefrontal cortex. Macmillan concluded that Gage's prefrontal cortex must have, in fact, regenerated. This led to the possibility of what we now know is the plasticity and ability of the prefrontal cortex to recover and grow. Gage's life is one of the topics well known to neurology students. The recovery of his prefrontal cortex should be considered by teachers to represent hope for students who lack or are delayed in developing executive function skills.

Making a Difference in the Classroom

The term *executive function* emerged in the 1980s, relatively recently in education history. Executive function encompasses a collection of skills related to working memory, inhibitory control, planning, organization, and higher-order reasoning. While once the focus of research into mental illness, it has come to also be associated with autism, attention deficit disorder (ADD), and attention deficit hyperactivity disorder (ADHD). Now, it is becoming more obvious that the skills that comprise executive function are the keys to academic achievement for all.

While scientific knowledge of the workings of the prefrontal cortex are relatively new, we now know that executive function skills are necessary for making sense of classroom instruction and that, through targeted experiences, teachers can contribute to the growth of the prefrontal cortex and executive function skills. Therefore, teachers can have a positive impact on student achievement by incorporating deliberate activities, structures, and facilitation strategies into the learning environment. For younger students, building foundational executive function skills will better position them to learn academic content. For older students who seem to have a strong foundation, continuing to focus on building executive function skills may save them from making some very detrimental decisions in their lives.

If a principal escorted a new student with a broken arm into class, the teacher would make adjustments to accommodate the learner, given the physiological deficit. No teacher would say, "try harder," instructing a student to reach an object with a broken arm. Likewise, the term "try harder" should not be applied to students with an underdeveloped prefrontal cortex. Telling a child who has memory problems to "try harder" is ineffective and harmful to a student's sense of self. Addressing deficits through deliberate activities and structures will yield far greater results in a relatively short period of time.

Where to Start

Rather than focusing on executive function skills as another content area to be mastered for its own sake, approach executive function skills from the perspective of their importance in building important life skills. While individual executive function skills are not exclusively used in one area of life, the categorizations below will offer a roadmap, if you will, for where to start when considering how to support executive function in students.

◆ **Conscious Control** (#EF_ConsciousControl)—One's success in life and human interaction is dependent upon one's ability to consciously control actions rather than being merely reactive. Being able to *focus, concentrate,* and *manage conflicting thoughts* are a few of the executive function skills related to conscious control.

◆ **Engagement** (#EF_Engagement)—Student compliance in the classroom may produce short-term results and the appreciation of teachers but not necessarily long-term learning. Students must grapple with content in order to make sense and meaning of it, a requirement of long-term retention of knowledge (Sousa, 2011). *Thinking about multiple concepts simultaneously, identifying cause-and-effect relationships,* and *persisting in a task* are a few of the executive function skills related to engagement.

◆ **Collaboration** (#EF_Collaboration)—Personal and professional advancement relies upon one's ability to work well with others, including working together to solve problems. Learning is social; it involves engaging with others and others' ideas; it is a process of give and take, and, as one collective mind, of moving beyond one's self to take ideas and innovations to the next level. *Seeing multiple sides to a situation, being open to others' points of view,* and *thinking before acting* are a few of the executive function skills related to collaboration.

◆ **Empowerment** (#EF_Empowerment)—With learning comes independence, a level of autonomy and self-determination that allows one to advocate for one's needs, desires, and ideas responsibly. As teachers give students greater responsibility, choice, and voice in the classroom, students need to be able to rise to the challenge. *Setting goals, managing time,* and *self-assessing* are a few of the executive function skills related to empowerment.

◆ **Efficacy** (#EF_Efficacy)—Learning eventually outfits one to carry out a plan of action, achieve goals, and make a difference. While empowerment comes from others, efficacy comes from a personal sense of one's ability to make a difference: an important quality of a world citizen. *Organizing actions and thoughts, creating mental images,* and *predicting outcomes* are a few of the executive function skills related to efficacy.

◆ **Leadership** (#EF_Leadership)—Ultimately, the learned lead others to achieve personal and collective goals. Leadership does not mean that one leads in every situation but that one can lead in some. It does not necessarily mean that one must take a formal leadership role but rather that one is able to informally lead others. Our world depends upon the development of effective, empathetic leaders. Realizing one's leadership ability is dependent upon all of the executive function skills presented in this book and on combining them in ways to reap the greatest benefits.

As you ponder this collection of executive function skills, please know that it is impossible to pin any executive function skill to just one of the life skills above. Most of the executive function skills are critical to several of the life skills. This categorization is intended to shift focus from attempting to teach these skills as an end goal and, rather, address executive function skills from a "big picture" lens by linking them to more formidable life skills.

Summary of the Power, Promise, and Pitfalls of Executive Function

◆ Executive function skills are powerful partners in the teaching and learning relationship; therefore, teachers should pay as much attention to building executive function as they do to designing great content lessons.

◆ Executive function skills are controlled in great part by the prefrontal cortex, an area of the brain that undergoes significant change throughout the first 25 years of life; therefore, teachers should consider growth states of the prefrontal cortex and address students' needs accordingly.

◆ Chronic stress has a negative effect on the development of the prefrontal cortex and, thus, executive function skills; therefore, teachers should take steps to recognize when stress is a factor in physiological brain development and should not assume that students have control over their executive function skills.

◆ The prefrontal cortex has the ability to grow and heal based on use; therefore, teachers should provide students with deliberate activities and structures to build executive function skills, which will, in turn, build the prefrontal cortex.

References

Barkley, R. (2012). *Executive functions: What they are, how they work, and why they evolved*. New York: Guilford Press.

Cooper-Kahn, J., Dietzel, L. (2008). *Late, lost, and unprepared: A parent's guide to helping children with executive functioning*. Bethesda, MD: Woodbine House.

Mischel, W. (2014). *The marshmallow test: Mastering self-control*. New York: Little, Brown and Company.

Sousa, D. (2011). *How the brain learns* (4th ed.) Thousand Oaks, CA: Corwin.

World Economic Forum. (2016). *The future of jobs: Employment, skills, and workforce strategy for the Fourth Industrial Revolution*. Geneva: World Economic Forum.

2

Attaining Conscious Control
(#EF_ConsciousControl)

At birth, human beings are reactive, controlled by the stimuli around them and their own immediate needs. A baby wakes up hungry and starts crying, then sees a spinning mobile over the crib and stops crying to watch the twirling stars. Newborn infants are stimulus-bound and impulsive (Zelazo, 2010), merely reacting to the world around them. They don't make decisions about what to observe; they simply observe whatever comes into their immediate line of sight. Their attention turns from one stimulus to another, based on whichever catches their attention. By the end of the first year of life, they become more purposeful in their actions. Babies who once could not *attend* to an object for more than a minute, if that, can now sustain *focus* for 1–2 minutes. By age two, they can *focus* on an object in spite of distracting noises. They mature from being merely reactive to being able to employ conscious control over their actions and thoughts. As they continue to grow, they can *attend* to a video for several minutes without losing *focus*, become potty trained, learn to refrain from throwing food, and build other good skills for which their parents are thankful.

Conscious control is the first step toward engaging with others and the outside world, and eventually, imagining and achieving a plan for one's life. Attaining conscious control means people are no longer held captive by events and others around them. They may suffer joy or disappointment, but they can craft their own response to it. Others may make comments they want to wildly applaud or vigorously refute, but they get to decide on the

Table 2.1 Executive Function Skills Related to Conscious Control

Working Memory	Storing and manipulating visual and verbal information	*Inhibitory Control*	Attending to a person or activity
	Identifying same and different		**Focusing**
	Remembering details		**Concentrating**
	Following multiple steps		**Thinking before acting**
	Holding on to information while considering other information		Initiating a task
			Persisting in a task
	Identifying cause-and-effect relationships		Maintaining social appropriateness
	Categorizing information		
Cognitive Flexibility	**Shifting focus from one event to another**	*Self Awareness*	Self-assessing
	Changing perspective		Overcoming temptation
	Seeing multiple sides to a situation		Monitoring performance
	Being open to others' points of view		Reflecting on goals
	Being creative		**Managing conflicting thoughts**
	Catching and correcting errors		
	Thinking about multiple concepts simultaneously		

best response. They have conscious control. Human beings develop conscious control as the prefrontal cortex grows, typically in the early years of life, building critical executive function skills.

The executive function skills human beings need to exhibit conscious control are listed here, along with the four related overarching executive function categories into which they fall (see also Table 2.1.):

- ◆ Attending to a person or activity (Inhibitory Control)
- ◆ Focusing (Inhibitory Control)
- ◆ Concentrating (Inhibitory Control)
- ◆ Thinking before acting (Inhibitory Control)
- ◆ Storing and manipulating visual and verbal information (Working Memory)
- ◆ Remembering details (Cognitive Flexibility)
- ◆ Shifting focus from one event to another (Cognitive Flexibility)
- ◆ Holding on to information while considering other information (Cognitive Flexibility)
- ◆ Managing conflicting thoughts (Self-Awareness).

As brain development continues, preschool children build significant levels of conscious control over their actions and thoughts, particularly between the ages of four and five. Executive function develops as a progression of increasingly complex cognitive processes:

Whereas a two-year-old can get her mind around a simple directive ('Put the red ones here'), a three-year-old is able to reflect on this directive and consider it in contrast to another directive: 'If it's red, put it here; but if it's blue, put it there'. That is, three-year-olds formulate a pair of rules. Four-year-olds can go one step further: they consider two incompatible pairs of rules and formulate a more general rule for choosing between them: 'If it's the colour game, then if it's red, put it here...' (Zelazo, 2010, May 31)

As students enter kindergarten, they typically have enough executive function for sufficient conscious control. They still need, however, to mature in this area, and some students may lag in the development of some of the executive function skills identified in Table 2.1. A student may have trouble sitting still, attending to the teacher, or keeping track of personal belongings. A student may call out, grab another student's belongings, or run from the classroom. All these situations are addressed by building the executive function skills for conscious control.

Students at higher grade levels who have executive dysfunction may also be lacking in the executive function skills for conscious control. For them, the challenge is that, because they are older, adults might assume they are being contrary or lazy. In fact, it may be that their prefrontal cortex has not sufficiently developed to allow them to have conscious control over their actions. Deliberate and purposeful actions on the part of educators will have a positive effect on students' brain development. The executive function skills related to conscious control can be fostered through both activities and structures.

Activities

Engage students in a variety of activities that help build the executive function skills they need to take conscious control of their thoughts and actions. Where possible, work to include activities into everyday learning across the content areas, as opposed to addressing executive function as a subject area unto itself. You most likely don't have time to add anything to the curriculum; you can address executive function skills alongside content studies. Consider how you might use the following activities, and invent or identify others that address the executive function skills for conscious control listed earlier in the chapter.

Now You See It; Now You Don't

This activity is useful for strengthening the executive function skills of *focusing* and *concentrating* in students of all ages. The idea is to have students look at an image and then, with the image removed from sight, attempt to remember as many details as possible. At the primary level, use simple drawings, such as colorful geometric shapes, and ask students to look at them for several seconds. Then, without the image in sight, ask students to recall details such as colors, shapes, and obvious characteristics. You can use this as a two-player activity as well, where one student shows the image and then hides it from the second student, who attempts to recall details while the first confirms them.

As students improve upon their recall skills, have them attempt to notice more of the details of the image. Ask students questions, such as: "What color is the mother's hair?" or "How many cars are on the bridge?" Students must *focus* on the image to discern all the details. As you incorporate a time limit for viewing, students must improve their ability to *concentrate* in order to take in as much as they can in a short period of time.

At the secondary level, use more complex images related to the content you are teaching, offering students a timed look at the picture followed by having them make a list of what they remembered. Students can then self check to see how much they remembered.

This simple memory activity builds the executive function skills of *attending to an activity, focusing, concentrating, storing and manipulating visual information*, and *remembering details*. Therefore, it's a great activity for exercising executive function related to conscious control. You can vary it in several ways, including having students select an image and write questions for their peers to attempt to answer.

Skill Visualization

Professional athletes use visualization to improve their performance. Golfers envision themselves swinging a club, skiers making a jump, swimmers racing through the pool, and so on. Sometimes they visualize their performance with eyes open, sometimes with eyes closed. Sometimes, rather than just thinking about the performance, they move their arms and legs and act as if they are engaged in their sport: skiing down a hill, riding in a luge, swinging a tennis racket, shooting a basketball, etc. In Olympic sports competitions, "the starting areas have been full of Olympians going through the motions, figuratively or literally. 'Oh, yeah, it's ridiculous; we're all up there flapping our arms,' [Olympic aerial skier Emily] Cook said. 'It looks insane, but it works'" (Clarey, C., Feb. 22, 2014). Olympic teams travel with sports psychologists to help them in their visualization.

Artistic performers use visualization to practice art, music, and performing arts. Visualizing a piano piece has been shown to reduce the actual practice time needed and improve a performance (Kageyama, N., n.d.).

That's not to say one should eliminate actual practice, but visualization is a powerful partner in the learning process. Parts of the brain cannot tell the difference between visualizing an experience or experiencing it. Visualization can provide focused practice; the act of closing one's eyes can shut out visual distractions.

Teachers can use visualization to help students work through academic skills and procedures. In a Small-Group Mini-Lesson, have students gather and stand around you while you demonstrate a skill, such as: balancing a chemical equation, drawing a bar graph, cutting with scissors, reading a graduated cylinder, conjugating an AR verb in Spanish, drawing in one-point perspective, etc. You can demonstrate the skill by writing on a board, using a presentation device, or using hands-on materials. Be deliberate in separating the skill into steps. Then ask students to close their eyes and visualize what they just saw while you verbally walk them through the skill. Slowly describe the process so that they can visualize it mentally. Then have them open their eyes. Demonstrate the skill again, walking them through the steps as you did when their eyes were closed. Then ask them to close their eyes and visualize it without you guiding them. Ask them how accurately they felt they visualized the skill. After several visualization practices, have them then attempt to perform the skill themselves, with their eyes open, sitting back down at a table if necessary.

Once students understand the visualization process, they can use a How-To Sheet, video, or other resource to identify the steps of a particular skill or performance. They can then first follow the steps while reading or listening to them, and then close their eyes to visualize. You can assign visualization practice for classwork or homework, telling students to be sure to find a quiet place where they can close their eyes and practice a skill without being distracted. Encourage students to stop and visualize themselves successfully achieving a task before they actually pursue it.

Visualization can strengthen students' ability to exhibit conscious control over their thoughts and actions related to academic content, building the executive function skills of: *attending to a person or activity*, *focusing*, *concentrating*, *storing and manipulating visual and verbal information*, *remembering details*, and *thinking before acting*. As students learn to block out distractions, they will also be exercising the skill of *managing conflicting thoughts*.

Fast Practice

Some academic content must be committed to memory, such as math facts, the alphabet (in a native or world language), vocabulary definitions, and so forth. Once students achieve accuracy in the content, challenge them to speed practice by adding a timer. This can add a fun challenge to the content practice and build the executive function skills of *focusing* and *concentrating*, as students will be more motivated to ignore distractions in order to achieve an improved time score. Begin with small chunks of easy content, for example, the multiplication facts up to two times a number. Offer a short time-frame for the students to see how many questions they can answer.

It is important, however, for students to learn the content first and then increase the speed of recall. Working on speed prior to mastering the content may produce anxiety and lead to lower achievement. Once a student can retrieve the information from memory, indicating mastery of the content, then you can add speed. As students build speed, you can add more difficult content; but never prioritize speed over accuracy or you may negatively impact learning. Point out to students: first demonstrate accuracy, then speed.

Games

Games are powerful for building executive function skills at all levels. With an increasing focus on subject-area content in schools, it's easy to classify games as being an added attraction or free-time activity; however, games play an important role in building executive function skills and should be deliberately integrated into the school day. While games such as chess build myriad higher-order executive function skills, this section will focus on some of the more well-known games for building executive function skills related to conscious control:

◆ Concentration—Matching pairs of cards (words, colors, images, numbers, playing cards, etc.) are shuffled and laid out in a grid. To start, use a four by four grid of just sixteen cards and increase the size as students build their skills. A student turns over any two cards. If the pair is a match, the student keeps the cards, otherwise the cards are turned back over. The key is for students to remember those revealed cards for future tries. Students may need to be cued to remember the cards so it does not become a game of continual chance. Students can play in pairs or triads, competing for the most pairs of cards, or alone, competing for the fewest number of turns to match all the cards. This game builds many executive function skills, including most of those related to conscious control: *attending to a person or activity, focus, concentrating, storing and manipulating visual and verbal information*, and *holding on to information while considering other information*. Concentration can be played with a set of purchased or playing cards. You can make sets of cards based on content, such as community helpers, landforms, or French nouns.

There are also a variety of online versions available. As students master the basic game, increase the number of cards and/or the identification difficulty, such as: matching numbers or multiples of the number (e.g., 2 and 6 would be considered a pair); matching words or parts of words (e.g., pat and patch would be considered a pair); or using a deck of playing cards and asking students to match either the number or the suit. This increases students' need for *holding on to information while considering other information* and *remembering details*.

◆ Playing-card games—Games played with a deck of playing cards can strengthen a variety of executive function skills. Some games involve remembering cards that are or are not in other players' hands (such as Go Fish, and, for older students, Rummy.) Some require a fast response, such as Slap Jack, Snap, and Speed. Playing-card games generally activate *focusing, concentrating, holding on to information while considering other information, storing and manipulating visual and verbal information*, and *thinking before acting*.

◆ At the time of this writing, www.quizlet.com was a popular website providing a variety of ways to practice matching terms to definitions, from matching letters of the alphabet to pictures to matching high-school level terms to definitions. You can design your own or search those created by others. The site provides a learning mode, flashcards, and games. One game, Scatter, fills the screen with terms (including pictures if you use them) and definitions. The object is to drag the term and corresponding definition onto one another so that they disappear. A timer provides an added incentive of beating your own or others' time. Again, these online game activities exercise most of the executive function skills necessary for conscious control.

In addition to the executive function skills addressed by specific games, the social engagement of games played by two or more students forces them to exercise the executive function skill of *managing conflicting thoughts*, such as wanting to quit prematurely.

Songs
While singing might be considered part of the music curriculum, it can also be a powerful activity for building foundational executive function skills. Learning to sing a song requires *focusing, attending to an activity, remembering details*, and *storing and manipulating visual and verbal information*. Older students can learn jingles to commercials to build executive function skills

while learning about the art of persuasion. Younger students can learn songs that build content, such as the alphabet song. Singing "Old Mac Donald," students must remember different animals and the sounds they make; with each verse, they repeat the previously mentioned animals and add a new one, with the repetition building their working memory.

Songs with rounds, such as "Row, Row, Row Your Boat," require students to *concentrate* on their part so that they sing that, rather than getting confused and switching to another part. Songs with rounds can be fun for any age level. In the beginning, divide the class in half and have one side start and then the other side. Then, divide the class into more groups for more rounds. As they improve, have the students mix so that they are all sitting next to others who are singing different rounds, thus challenging them to *concentrate*.

Add movement to songs so that students have to remember and retrieve words and actions. Like "Musical Chairs," play music and have students sing along with movement. Stop the music in the midst and give students a "freeze" movement to follow, such as standing on one leg, arms overhead, etc. You can model the movement or use large pictures of stick figures to hold up when the music stops. This musical-movement interaction will build executive function and provide a fun exercise break. It also strengthens the executive function skills of *thinking before acting* and *holding on to information while considering other information*.

Songs tend to be a part of students' age-related culture, with knowledge of certain songs and artists often defining a generation. They are, therefore, a natural venue for building the necessary executive function skills to attain conscious control.

Playing Musical Instruments

Learning to play a musical instrument builds many executive function skills and most of those related to conscious control, including: *attending to an activity*, *focusing*, *concentrating*, *storing and manipulating visual and verbal information*, and *remembering details*. Research indicates that musicians demonstrate somewhat higher degrees of executive function than non-musicians, particularly in the area of working memory (Zuk, J., Benjamin, C., Kenyon, A., & Gaab, N., 2014). While encouraging students to take lessons in a musical instrument can be a definite benefit to building executive function, you can have students play simple musical instruments in class as well. The recorder is an inexpensive, easy-to-learn instrument that allows students to practice and play, thus building the foundational executive function skills to attain conscious control. Certainly, playing an instrument demonstrates conscious control in a very concrete way. In higher grades, students could include the playing of music in the context of their studies by, for example, providing the musical background for a multimedia presentation. I once had a group of middle school orchestra students each code their parts into computers to play the music digitally. The group attempted to hit the enter key on each computer at the same time to create their digital orchestra. Their continual reflection, error correction, and persistence was powerful. In the end, they succeeded!

Conversation Swap

Have students work in pairs or triplets for this activity. One student (the talker) identifies two different conversational topics, such as weekend activities and a favorite vacation. The talker begins to talk about one conversation while the other students become listeners. After a short period of time, one of the listeners says, "swap," and the talker must start talking about the other topic. After a bit of listening, one of the listeners says, "swap," and the talker must continue talking about the first topic, without repeating what was already said. The students continue to swap the conversation to see how long the talker can continue without repeating information or losing the train of thought. While it may be difficult for the listeners to accurately determine if there has been repetition in the conversation, the activity is challenging, and fun, and it emphasizes the skill of *shifting focus from one event to another* along with other executive function skills. At first, the talker will most likely get confused after a few swaps. S/he will start building internal strategies to keep track of the conversation, such as telling the events chronologically, *creating mental images*, silently repeating a cue word a few times before the swap, etc. Once students master the general strategy for swapping their conversations, you can focus them on curricular content. Have them talk about different books they have read, different subjects they are studying, different biomes, and so forth.

Secondary students can discuss literature, historic events, art critiques, and more in this manner, switching between those with different points of view. For example, a student talking about World War I could represent both Serbia and Austria-Hungary, swapping back and forth to present the buildup of animosity that led to the war; a student talking about a work of art could swap between the artist's perspective and a critic's perspective; and so forth. While students would generally study this, taking notes and reporting it back on a test; a Conversation Swap truly requires them to understand the content and *focus* their thoughts and statements. This can be a useful activity for prepping for a test, swapping between two aspects of the content.

Conversation Swap exercises all the foundational executive function skills for conscious control. Given you can have students engage in conversations around content students are learning, you can build those executive function skills while having students strengthen their knowledge of the subject area content.

The Birdwalking Challenge

Have you ever watched birds walk around? They dart in one direction and then the other with seemingly no deliberate plan. In a conversation, when the speaker veers off the topic to interject an unrelated or unnecessary comment or story, it's called birdwalking. As an example:

Student One: So, you can find solar panels on the roofs of houses and buildings.

Student Two: And sometimes they're installed on the ground.

Student One: I've seen them on, like, street lights or signs, so I guess they power them.

Student Two: My neighbors heat their pool water through solar panels on the roof. It's really cool; the pipes run up over the roof and back down.

Student One: Which one of your neighbors has a pool?

The brain stores and retrieves information by association. While the conversation is about solar energy, Student One hears the word pool and starts thinking about a pool rather than solar panels. With strong executive function, the student would dismiss the distraction and remain focused on the content of the conversation; however, even adults struggle with this skill as it requires great self-discipline. Sometimes a speaker or writer will interject a humorous comment just to get the laugh, when the comment is not essential to the conversation or text. Sometimes a speaker or writer will interject a personal anecdote that is not essential to the conversation or text just to attract attention. Intermediate and secondary students can be taught to *focus* on others' and their own conversations with the goal of recognizing and avoiding birdwalking.

Introduce students to the concept of birdwalking and ask them to challenge one another when they detect the conversation is going off topic. When students are working in groups, make one of the roles the Birdwalk Manager, responsible for alerting the group when they shift off topic. You might establish a hand signal of some sort, such as a T for time-out, to indicate the speaker is birdwalking.

This activity exercises all the executive function skills necessary for attaining conscious control. It particularly emphasizes the skill of *managing conflicting thoughts* for the speaker while emphasizing skills in *attending, focusing,* and, *concentrating* for the listeners.

Other Activities

Be mindful of the executive function skills related to conscious control listed at the beginning of this chapter and deliberately build opportunities for students to strengthen them. Make students aware of the list of target skills; older students may identify or invent activities on their own to build skills.

Structures

In addition to engaging students in activities, you can use various structures to support conscious control. Combine these structures with academic goals, using them throughout the day.

Focus Card

For young students and those with weak executive function, the Focus Card helps to build the executive function skill of *focusing* and, thus, staying on task: critical skills for attaining conscious control. Each student has a card (see Table 2.2) to keep nearby while working. During the day or class period, signal your students to stop and decide how well they are *focusing* on their work. The students fill in the time and then check one of the three columns.

You can then review the results with students or have them share with one another. They can share why they rated themselves in the way they did. Making students aware of how well they are *focusing* on their work is a great first step to building the skill of *focusing*.

The Talk Stick

Group discussions can be challenging when students lack the executive function skills related to conscious control. Students may call out; their comments may not be related to the topic; they may disengage when someone else is speaking; etc. In order to help students learn to *attend to a person, focus, shift focus from one event to another* in a discussion, and *think before acting*, use a Talk

Table 2.2 Focus Card

Time	I'm really not doing my best	I'm doing okay	I'm impressing myself

Stick. You may already use something similar. Designate a stick, perhaps wrapped in yarn or colorful tape to make it easily visible. During a group discussion, the student with the stick is the only one allowed to talk. Others must *focus* on the speaker until the speaker passes the stick to another student. For large groups use a soft foam ball or something similar that can be tossed around to group members without causing injury. The Talk Stick is a simple structure to cue students to exercise executive function.

As students build the ability to *attend* and engage in a discussion, wean them off the Talk Stick. The purpose of this structure is to draw attention on the skills of *attending, focusing, shifting focus,* and *thinking before acting*. Given that, in actual conversations in which they'll engage in life, students will not use a Talk Stick, it's important to use this structure only as a cue to make them aware of their behavior as they build executive function. Deliberately address the goal of being able to have a conversation without needing the Talk Stick, demonstrating a level of increased conscious control.

Silent Discussion

If you've ever engaged in a Twitter chat, you know how intense it can be, with others putting out questions and comments, and you attempting to read it all and contribute. It's a great representation of a silent discussion. Cloud-based technology allows you to engage students in a closed online discussion or blog (meaning it's available only to your students or whomever you allow in) in which they engage through writing instead of talking. At the time of this writing, www.todaysmeet.com was one online discussion room option, though you could also use a blogging or discussion feature of your cloud-based software.

One advantage to the Silent Discussion is that shy students can contribute more easily; and each student can add a lot more to the conversation because they can all be typing at the same time. From an executive function standpoint, students need to *focus* and *concentrate* on the conversation, *shift focus from one event to another*, in terms of conversation threads, and *hold onto information while considering other information*. It can be a fun but challenging discussion experience, strengthening executive function in the process.

While you can create discussions asynchronously, meaning students can open the file and add to it at any time, reading what others wrote at a different time; the value of the silent discussion is when a group is all reading and writing at the same time, engaged in a synchronous, or live, discussion. Start small, with a pair (younger grades) or group of four to ensure students build the skill of reading and writing. Then expand the group as students build their skills. Your students can also enjoy a Silent Discussion with students from other classrooms and schools if you want to set it up that way.

Ordering Activities

If students have several activities or assignments to complete during a work session, have them order them in advance, and then follow that order. Suppose a first-grade student has to practice recognizing words from a word list, engage in buddy reading, and write a journal entry. Having the student order the activities with a 1, 2, and 3 does more to build executive function than simply letting them complete any one, then move to any other, or telling students which to complete, first, second, and last. As students complete an activity, they must, on their own, *shift focus from one event to another* that they decided in advance; they must *think before acting*, ensuring they are following their ordered list. They may have to *manage conflicting thoughts* if they finished the first and would rather work on the third than the second, which they originally chose. Allowing students to order a small number of activities and then address them in that order will strengthen several of the executive function skills of conscious control. For older students, consider developing a longer list of activities to cover the day or, for secondary students, the week, allowing them to schedule how they will use their time to achieve learning goals.

Summary for Attaining Conscious Control (#EF_ConsciousControl)

Consider the executive function skills required and built by students' development of conscious control. See how many activities and structures you can build into the day to enhance students' skills toward moving beyond being reactive to taking control of their own behaviors, thoughts, and actions.

Executive Function Skills:

◆ Attending to a person or activity
◆ Focusing
◆ Concentrating
◆ Thinking before acting
◆ Storing and manipulating visual and verbal information
◆ Remembering details
◆ Shifting focus from one event to another
◆ Holding on to information while considering other information
◆ Managing conflicting thoughts

Activities:

- ◆ Now You See It; Now You Don't
- ◆ Visualization
- ◆ Fast Practice
- ◆ Games
- ◆ Songs
- ◆ Playing Musical Instruments
- ◆ Conversation Swap
- ◆ Birdwalk Challenge.

Structures:

- ◆ Focus Card
- ◆ Talk Stick
- ◆ Ordering Activities.

References

Clarey, C. (2014, February 22). Olympians use imagery as mental training. *The New York Times*, Retrieved from http://www.nytimes.com/2014/02/23/sports/olympics/olympians-use-imagery-as-mental-training.html

Kageyama, N. (n.d.). Does mental practice work? Retrieved from: http://www.bulletproofmusician.com/does-mental-practice-work/

Zelazo, P. D. (2010, May 31). Executive function part two: The development of executive function in infancy and childhood. Retrieved from http://www.aboutkidshealth.ca/En/News/Series/ExecutiveFunction/Pages/Executive-Function-Part-Two-The-development-of-executive-function-in-infancy-and-early-childhood.aspx

Zuk, J., Benjamin, C., Kenyon, A., and Gaab, N. (2014). Behavioral and Neural Correlates of Executive Functioning in Musicians and Non-Musicians. *PLoS ONE*, 9(6): e99868. doi:10.1371/journal.pone.0099868.

Moving from Compliance
to Engagement
(#EF_Engagement)

You've probably seen it at some point, in or out of school: students who are so engrossed in a challenge that they lose all track of time and the world around them. They are inquisitive and dogged in their search for answers, passionate about their outcomes, joyful in the pursuit of learning, and persistent. It might be a student playing a video game, learning a musical piece, building a fort from boxes, programming a robot, or designing a habitat for an animal. According to The Glossary of Education Reform (2016), "student engagement refers to the degree of attention, curiosity, interest, optimism, and passion that students show when they are learning or being taught, which extends to the level of motivation they have to learn and progress in their education." Learning requires engaging with concepts, skills, and information in a way that mesmerizes and transforms students, such that they do not want to stop until they succeed.

Engagement leads to learning, that is, understanding and retention of content; it is no wonder it is a key goal for most schools. Far too many students in classrooms today are either disengaged and, thus, exhibit behavioral problems or are compliantly carrying out teachers' directives, doing what they are told. Neither situation leads to lasting learning. To move students beyond mere compliance, employ strategies, structures, and programs that foster student engagement with content.

Years ago, a colleague of mine was working with a fourth-grade teacher in an underperforming school. The teacher felt that she could not use problem-based learning in her classroom because her students demonstrated too many behavior problems. The consultant convinced her to try it, with him working alongside her. They introduced a problem-based task dealing with measurement, offered up some parameters and learning opportunities, and set the students to work. The classroom was transformed, with students engaged in trying to solve the problem. After a while, the consultant asked the teacher what she thought. She had to admit that the behavior problems were gone (typically, engaged students don't have the time or interest in misbehaving). She said, however, she didn't think they were actually learning, just having fun. The consultant had one of the early digital cameras that stored images on a disk. He started taking pictures. With 10 minutes to spare, he stopped the class, loaded the images into the computer, and began showing one image at a time, asking the students what was going on at that moment. Students spoke excitedly about the project, used appropriate math terms, and demonstrated their understanding of the content. The teacher was convinced: engagement was a better goal than the compliance she was struggling to attain.

Alternatively, there are many high-achieving schools where students can read a text, make sense of it, and perform well on a test. These students compliantly move through their days waiting for the final bell to ring so they can get on with their lives. I've sat in classrooms where students stream in, open their notebooks, and begin working on whatever the teacher has on the board. Once the teacher starts presenting content, they look, listen, and write in their notebooks. When asked a closed-ended question, some raise their hands with the answer. I was in one classroom where students would look around as if they were seeing if anyone else was going to answer; if not, a student would raise a hand and comply. The teacher, focused on presenting content, thought it was a good class period. If you focused instead on what was going on inside students' heads and how engaged they were in grappling with content, the class period fell far short as a powerful learning experience.

Whether students are behavior problems, perfectly compliant, or somewhere in between, teachers must shift to expecting engagement and creating the conditions for student engagement to take place. Students who have mastered the executive function skills of achieving conscious control, as defined in Chapter 2, may be able to be compliant in that they will be able to focus, sit still, and pay attention. However, schools must embrace the importance of engagement in the learning process and ensure that students build the executive function skills to engage purposefully and meaningfully in learning activities.

In his book, *Rethinking Education: Learning in the New Renaissance*, Stephen Murgatroyd (2011) offers four distinct characteristics of an engaged learner:

- ◆ The student sees the activity as personally meaningful.
- ◆ The student's level of interest is sufficiently high that he persists in the face of difficulty.
- ◆ The student finds the task sufficiently challenging that she believes she will accomplish something of worth by doing it.
- ◆ The student's emphasis is on optimum performance and on "getting it right." (2011, p. 116)

Consider students who are engrossed in a video game, engaged in learning how to reach successive levels. Most likely, the above characteristics would apply to them. These engaged students possess the executive function skills of *initiating* and *persisting in a task*, thus their seeming captivation with the game. They can *follow multiple steps* to learning the game, including the additional steps often needed to achieve at higher levels of the game. They can *think about multiple concepts simultaneously* as they grapple with the challenges, requirements, scoring, and obstacles of the game. As they engage with the game, they can *identify same and different* and *categorize information* in order to discern helpful components from distracting or detrimental components as they navigate their way to success. They can *identify cause-and-effect relationships* and *change perspective* as they analyze the situation and take different actions to succeed. You can apply these same skills to any situation in which you find students fully engaged; these are the executive function skills of engagement.

You can utilize specific activities and structures to build the executive function skills that support engagement. As you consider those presented in this chapter, you will no doubt generate other ideas. It might be a matter of taking an existing activity or structure and modifying it slightly to focus deliberately on one or more of the target skills. As you read through the ideas presented in this chapter, keep in mind these executive function skills that support engagement with content (also see Table 3.1.):

- ◆ Identifying same and different (Working Memory)
- ◆ Following multiple steps (Working Memory)
- ◆ Identifying cause-and-effect relationships (Working Memory)
- ◆ Categorizing information (Working Memory)
- ◆ Changing perspective (Cognitive Flexibility)
- ◆ Thinking about multiple concepts simultaneously (Cognitive Flexibility)
- ◆ Initiating a task (Inhibitory Control)
- ◆ Persisting in a task (Inhibitory Control).

Table 3.1 Executive Function Skills Related to Engagement

Working Memory	Storing and manipulating visual and verbal information	*Inhibitory Control*	Attending to a person or activity
	Identifying same and different		Focusing
	Remembering details		Concentrating
	Following multiple steps		Thinking before acting
	Holding on to information while considering other information		**Initiating a task**
			Persisting in a task
	Identifying cause-and-effect relationships		Maintaining social appropriateness
	Categorizing information		
Cognitive Flexibility	Shifting focus from one event to another		
	Changing perspective		
	Seeing multiple sides to a situation		
	Being open to others' points of view		
	Being creative		
	Catching and correcting errors		
	Thinking about multiple concepts simultaneously		

Activities

In addition to providing a content lesson with materials for students on a concept or skill, plan activities that focus on building executive function skills for engagement. Unlike the predominantly, stand-alone activities for building the executive function skills of conscious control (Chapter 2), activities that focus on engagement tend to be embedded into the study of the content. Following are ideas for activities teachers can incorporate into their content lessons to build these executive function skills.

Focusing on Perspectives

Philosopher René Descartes described intelligence as having two components: perspicacity (the ability to see multiple perspectives and gain insights) and sagacity (wisdom derived from analyzing trends over time.) While both are highly valued, higher-order skills, they begin with, among others, the simple executive function skill of the ability to *change perspectives*: an executive function skill that paves the way for greater engagement with content.

To gain an understanding of place value, students must be able to *change perspective* from viewing a collection of objects as single units to viewing them also as groups of ten. To build empathy critical to the engineering design process, students must be able to *change perspective* from their view of a situation to that of another. To understand point of view in writing, students must be able to *change perspective*, for example, from that of a person telling her story to a person telling the story on her behalf.

Teachers can build perspective activities into any subject area and grade level. At the earliest levels, consider something as simple as an apple. Describe what it looks like if you look at just the top, then just the bottom, then the side. Then cut it open and describe what it looks like on the inside. Have students explore a variety of objects by looking down on them to looking eye level at them to, where appropriate, cutting them open. Challenging the brain to view an object from different perspectives while making sense of the fact that it is the same object will strengthen the skill of *changing perspective*. Secondary art students learn to draw in different perspectives, looking at a building, for example, from an angle off to the side or from above or below. Many computer programs and applications today allow the user to view and rotate an object to observe it from all perspectives.

Exploring perspectives from a physical standpoint is a first step in being able to *change perspective* regarding concepts, such as different perspectives in a revolution or civil war, different ways of looking at data, or different perspectives on the value of electric cars. For students to build toward the higher-order ability to identify unintended consequences, an important skill in decision-making, they must be able to look at a situation from multiple perspectives.

As you consider your content, what are the various perspectives through which students could consider it? Provide opportunities for students to explore and identify perspectives. Some may seem more obvious. Ask students to consider the different perspectives of an event by different characters. The launch of the first satellite, Sputnik, by Russia was viewed very differently by Russians as compared to Americans. Why? Ask young students to draw or write about the perspective of the world as a caterpillar and then as a butterfly. The caterpillar will mostly see leaves; the butterfly will see the landscape from above and hone in on flowers. How would a landscape be viewed differently by an abstract artist and a photorealist? Most likely the abstract artist will see colors and shapes emerging; the photorealist will see details right down to the blades of grass. Ask students to consider content from different perspectives.

You can identify perspectives for almost any content. For example, the sound of the initial consonant "c" is different based on the subsequent letter. A simple activity is to have students hold different letter cards. One student holds the "c" card and considers the sound he would make if he were followed by the student with the "a" card. The teacher can ask, "How do you sound?" Then replace the second student holding the "a" card with the student holding the "e" card, and ask "How do you sound now? Give me some words that are examples." Then replace the second student with the one with the "h" card. Having students physically role-play the letter allows them to see that the "c" is the same letter, but it sounds different based on the movement of their peers representing the letter that follows, offering them another glimpse into perspective. While most primary teachers certainly engage in having students consider the sound of a consonant based on the letter that follows, the nuance here is a focus on perspective rather than the letter sound. While the activity is reinforcing content, the goal is to keep *changing perspective* from one situation to the next and back again so the student sees that the reason the sound, in this case, is changing is due to seeing the letter from a different perspective. This is a different activity from having students work with just letter combinations that make the hard "c" sound and then later working with just letter combinations that make the soft "c" sound. That activity focuses on the content of the sound of consonants and is appropriate for that purpose. Much of building executive function is about nuanced changes in the way you present or reinforce content in order to deliberately focus on executive function skills.

The study of prepositions opens the door for a discussion on perspectives, as most prepositions represent a relationship of perspective: around, in, under, on, over, between, etc. Have one student hold up a card with the name of an item, such as a book; have another hold up a card with the name of another item, such as a table. The rest of the class members become prepositions, each moving between the two so that the two students then have to use their cards to demonstrate the relationship between them based on the preposition. For example, when the preposition is "under," the student holding the first item card holds it lower than that of the second item; when the preposition is "around," the student walks around the student holding the other card. As students work through this activity, point out how the preposition changed the perspective of the items toward one another. This activity of physically demonstrating perspective can be modified to address other content.

In working with fractions, the power of the number in the position of numerator is different, depending on the denominator. Initially, when students see 2/3 and 5/8, they might assume the second fraction is larger because both the numerator and denominator of the second fraction are larger than the first, when, in fact, the first quantity is larger. Choosing 5/8 as the larger number could be attributed to the fact that students who are learning about fractions are used to the perspective of whole numbers. With fractions, however, the power of the number 2 in the numerator is based on the perspective of the denominator. If you're looking at eighths of a whole, you have a different perspective than looking at thirds of a whole. You could have a bag of coins, but the value will depend on whether you're holding a bag of pennies or a bag of silver dollars. Viewing that same bag from different perspectives is important.

Consider Piaget's famous experiment on the theory of conservation, which states that the basic properties of an object do not change when the object changes form. He worked with young children, showing them a glass of water. He would then pour that glass of water into a tall, thin cylinder. When asked which one had more water, the glass or the cylinder, children below the age of five generally chose the cylinder. Piaget noted that the ability to see that both vessels held the same amount of water developed beyond the age of five, due to brain development. Piaget's contributions to education occurred decades before anyone was even researching executive function and the prefrontal cortex. One aspect of developing Piaget's concept of conservation is building the executive function skill of *changing perspective*.

A valuable life lesson is understanding that everything may not always be as it seems; it must be viewed from different perspectives, and that requires executive function. Build in your students the habit of asking themselves, "can I view this in another way?"

For older students, offer opportunities to look at a situation or item from different perspectives. In reading literature, it might be describing the situation from the perspective of the protagonist and then from the perspective of the antagonist. In history, students can view a particular event from the different social science perspectives: geographic, political, economic, sociological, psychological, and cultural. Use a chart or have students role play each of the perspectives as they work to see a situation from the different perspectives. In Nathaniel Hawthorne's novel, *The Scarlet Letter*, students can react to the novel from the perspective of Hester Prynne, whose adultery was punished by having her wear a scarlet "A" on her clothing; Arthur Dimmesdale, the Puritan minister who struggles to keep the secret that he fathered Hester's illegitimate child; and the members of society during this period in Colonial America. Students could also view the events of the story in terms of the perspectives of today's society, even across various cultures and countries. While it may seem that high school students have the executive function skills to *change perspective*, consider that the prefrontal cortex of the brain does not fully develop until a person's mid-twenties; some of the challenges teens face in making decisions that are in their best interest require their ability to look at a decision from different perspectives.

Fostering Categorization Skills

You're headed out on a quiet vacation and want to buy some books to read. What types of books do you like? Mystery? Fantasy? Historical Fiction? Biography? Romance? As you just read that list, you may have had a reaction to one or more of the words in terms of how much you like or dislike that type of book. You may have thought of some books or authors you associate with each category. Books are classified using categories, making it easier to identify possible titles that might interest us. Libraries and book stores group books into categories, and those categories help the reader in decision-making and resource management. Human beings organize items, skills, concepts, and people into categories. There are categories to describe and organize rocks, paint colors, chemical elements, numbers, words, songs, governments, coding commands, and so forth. While it's easy to take this skill for granted, not all students have acquired this skill or can transfer it to academic settings, yet in order to engage with content, students will need the executive function skill of *categorizing information.*

As young children explore the world around them, they learn that apples, bananas, and grapes are all fruits; spinach, carrots, and lettuce are all vegetables. As they continue their exploration in school, they learn that hill, mountain, plateau, ridge, and valley are mountainous landforms; bay, channel, cape, inlet, and peninsula are oceanic landforms. Green, heavy, loud, and soft are adjectives; quickly, seldom, slowly, and very are adverbs. They learn in math class that two, three, five, seven, and eleven are prime numbers; four, six, eight, and nine are composite numbers. Armed with that information, they can solve more advanced calculation problems. Students *categorize* foods as dairy, fruits, grains, proteins, and vegetables in order to develop a new dinner entree in culinary arts class. Fluorine, chlorine, bromine, iodine, and astatine are halogens in the periodic table; helium, neon, and argon are among the noble gases. Categorization of elements provides a better understanding of the periodic table and the likelihood of element combinations. Blue, yellow, and red are primary colors; chartreuse, teal, and violet are tertiary colors. Fine artists and graphic artists find this information useful as they combine colors. Categorization is not limited to items; it can be used to organize concepts as well, such as the literary periods of romanticism, transcendentalism, realism, naturalism, and existentialism. The power of categorization transcends the disciplines.

Some people sort mail into piles, canned goods into groupings in the cabinet, and digital documents into folders in the cloud. *Categorization* is a tool used to organize information; we use it on a daily basis. It is an executive function skill under the category of Working Memory. *Categorizing information* helps in memorization, building understanding of content, and making meaning. It helps in building a foundation for new content. You'll find categorization of content in every subject area in school; and it is important to provide students with opportunities to *categorize* and think about how one develops categories.

Engagement with content involves grappling: mentally working with that content, turning it around in one's head, asking questions and seeking answers, generating ideas and seeing if they hold true. *Categorizing information* allows the brain to make sense of it, compare it with other information, and apply it to situations based on its characteristics. For example, if students are planning a food drive for financially challenged families in the school, with the intent of creating packages for people to take home over a holiday, they need to consider the various food categories. As foods arrive, they need to *categorize* them as fruits, vegetables, meats, starches, etc. They need to then consider how to select foods to make a nutritional package to send home. Engagement with content is enhanced when students possess particular executive function skills, of which one is categorization.

Graphic organizers are great tools for helping students build skill in *categorizing information*; several are already common practice. The food plate (formerly food pyramid) *categorizes* foods in terms of nutrition type. The periodic table classifies elements according to atomic makeup. Geography is studied through five themes. Maslow's Hierarchy uses a triangle to *categorize* human needs from the most basic to those of the highest level of self-actualization. Students can use tables to sort information into categories. They can use concentric rings to classify items related to concepts that expand on one another, such as self, local community, county, state, national, and global. Students can work through text and color code like items, such as statements that support an argument versus those that challenge it. For young students, sorting items into bins, folders, and piles will give them a more concrete experience through which to build understanding.

Rather than looking to address *categorization* as a discrete skill in a lesson plan, engage students in categorization across the subject areas, based on the content. Continually ask yourself where the subject area content you are addressing lends itself to categorization.

There are many computer applications as well that will provide students with experience in moving objects around the screen to *categorize* them. Using a spreadsheet, students can graph and visually see the results of categorization. For example, students might add up the various colors of candies in a bag and graph the results. You can also enter data in a spreadsheet and then sort it. For example, have students describe a collection of minerals, entering a line on a spreadsheet for each, noting hardness, luster, color, streak, cleavage, and fracture. They can then sort to see the number and types of minerals by category.

Categorization tends to build toward greater understanding of content in progressive years. Primary students, for example, might categorize leaves. In Table 3.2, they take 20 leaves and sort them first by shape, then by edges, then by type. At this level, they might explore how leaves are different based on where they are from.

Table 3.2

Take 20 leaves and sort them for each category.
Write down the number of leaves in each category.

Leaf Shape

Lobed	*Simple*

Leaf Edges

Smooth	*Toothed*

Leaf Type

Needle-Like	*Wide*

As students move into higher grades, they can begin to build *cause-and-effect relationships* (discussed in the next section) to learn that leaves in different climates have different characteristics. In areas with a winter season, trees tend to have leaves that are wider with greater surface area; many are lobed with toothed edges, promoting early photosynthesis, which makes sense since they have a shorter season for creating energy. Leaves in tropical areas are rarely lobed or toothed, and tend to have less surface area due to the abundance of sunlight available to them year-round. Early ability to *categorize* leads to a deeper understanding as the content becomes more complex. Scientists study leaf imprints in fossils in order to determine climate patterns across the years. All this begins with the executive function skills of *categorization* and *cause-and-effect relationships*.

Secondary students may *categorize* types of characters in novels to better understand how the author uses character types to build a story. Table 3.3 is an example of a graphic organizer for categorizing characters in a novel. As they grow in their understanding of characters and novel writing, they

Table 3.3 Categorization of Characters

Novel: _____

Character	Major	Minor		Dynamic	Static		Round	Flat		Direct Presentation	Indirect Presentation

will be able to make connections among character types and analyze why authors portray characters differently. They can expand on their understanding of character types in their own fiction writing.

As students build the executive function skill of *categorization of information* based on predetermined categories, teachers can prompt them to determine the categories they could use to organize content. For example, high school sociology students could be asked to consider how a sociologist might *categorize* people for the purpose of further study; they might arrive at categories such as female, male, child, adult, college educated, elderly, etc. Elementary students learn that matter is divided into three categories: solid, liquid, and gas. Chemistry teachers can ask students to consider how matter might be classified based on chemistry, which would lead them to elements that are metals or non-metals, compounds that are organic or inorganic, etc. Determining the categories themselves is an important and more rigorous application of the executive function skill of *categorization of information*.

Building the Concept of Cause-and-Effect Relationships

Everyday life is filled with *cause-and-effect* relationships. If you boil water, it will turn to steam; if you mix red and blue paint, you will produce purple; if you close your eyes tightly, you will not be able to see. Mastering this concept and using it strategically can lead to great success in life and career, as it is an important foundational skill for engagement with content and, relatedly, solving real-world problems.

Given that engagement with content requires the ability to grapple with it, the ability to see how one action can cause another action and another action becomes an increasingly important skill. I was in a middle-school classroom where students were studying the world water shortage and working in pairs to develop prototypes for irrigation systems. Before the teacher poured the cup of water into the one end of the prototype for testing, he asked the class for feedback for the designers. Students offered up several suggestions, all based on their ability to identify *cause-and-effect* relationships: the slope of the pipe flattened out too much and would cause water to collect; a particular stretch of pipeline was not adequately supported and might collapse with the weight of the water; etc. The designers then had 2 minutes to make any adjustments.

Primary students reading the book, *If You Give a Mouse a Cookie* (Numeroff, 2005), can draw a wonderful set of *cause-and-effect relationships* as the cookie causes the mouse to ask for milk, which causes him to ask for a straw, and then a mirror to avoid a milk moustache, and then nail scissors to trim his hair that he now sees in the mirror, and so forth. Acquiring each subsequent item causes him to need another item. Still, following the chain requires the concept of *cause-and-effect relationships*.

Fifth-grade students shared with me how they were developing a food web and considering the impact of the loss of certain species; that requires knowledge of *cause-and-effect relationships*. Kindergarten students explained to me that the rain and sun helps plants grow. I listened to chemistry students grapple with creating a better pottery glaze, discussing the effects of mixing different alkaline and acidic oxides.

In order to grapple with content to gain understanding, students need to understand *cause-and-effect relationships*. The good news is that they exist practically everywhere; and they're not limited to academic content. *Cause-and-effect relationships* play an important role in making good behavioral decisions as well, whether for an upset kindergarten student who wants to throw a toy or a high school senior deciding whether or not to drink alcohol at the pre-prom party. Thus, working to build the executive function skill of *identifying cause-and-effect relationships* will help your students in their academics and their daily lives.

As you consider your content, note *cause-and-effect relationships* that exist and draw your students' attention to them. Students can use a simple graphic organizer like the one in Figure 3.1 to fill in an action or feeling on the left and the effect of it on the right.

For example: fire causes heat; adding numbers creates larger numbers; adding water to watercolors causes the color to appear lighter; scarcity of goods causes an increase in price; blowing harder on a saxophone causes the

Figure 3.1

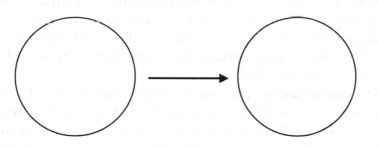

sound to be louder, practicing math facts leads to remembering math facts; persistence leads to success; calling someone a derogatory name causes hurt, and so forth.

Think through the subject area content or behavior you are looking to teach. For students with significant executive function deficits, begin by generating a collection of coaster-sized discs with causes written in one set (one cause per disc) and effects written in another set (one effect per disc), allowing students to attempt to match the *cause-and-effect* pairs.

Once students have a concept of *cause-and-effect*, they can use the diagramming tool (Figure 3.1) to map a primary *cause-and-effect* relationship on their own: primary meaning a specific cause produces a specific effect. For example, excessive rain causes flooding, success causes pride, friction causes heat. Encourage students to look for *cause-and-effect* relationships when exploring subject area content, reading stories, watching television shows, playing an instrument, practicing a sport, and more. Have them keep a *cause-and-effect* log and share their findings with one another. There are several computer applications that allow you to diagram as well, making it easy for students to build more complex *cause-and-effect* diagrams and easily change them if they make a mistake.

Coding, or the programming of objects, whether robotic or on-screen, is an excellent activity for building *cause-and-effect relationships*. For example, students provide the codes, or directions, to move an object from one location to another, navigating obstacles along the way. In doing so, they must consider the effect of each line of code to ensure the object will move to the correct destination. You can offer students a content-related coding project. One website that helps teachers get started is code.org. The Hour of Code activities offer a wealth of ideas and easy-to-use online coding applications for students.

While *identifying cause-and-effect relationships* often begins with the cause, the process can also begin with the effect. For example, gorillas are now listed as endangered. The population decline for gorillas is an effect that can be traced back to causes. It turns out that bushmeat, the meat of gorillas, is a popular food among the wealthy in urban centers of Africa. The increase in hunting for an animal that does not reproduce quickly causes a decline in the population. Thus, the increase in hunting for gorilla meat has caused a decline in the population of gorillas, but identifying the relationship, in this case, began with the end effect.

Civilizations tended to settle on the banks of rivers. Why? Students can deduce many of the causes of that effect: they arrived at new areas via the waterway and settled there; they had available water for irrigation of crops; they had a transportation route nearby; if they needed to hunt for animals, most likely the animals would head to the river for water. Again, it is the effect that leads students to consider the possible causes. Engage students in *identifying cause-and-effect relationships* that begin with the cause and those that are best analyzed by beginning with the effect.

Once students have a grasp of simple *cause-and-effect* relationships, they can grapple with secondary and tertiary *cause-and-effect* relationships. For example: heavy rain causes surface water runoff (primary effect) which causes soil erosion (secondary effect.) Figure 3.2 simply expands upon Figure 3.1 by an additional effect. You can continue to add circles to represent tertiary and quaternary effects.

Dust storms in the Sahara Desert propel sand particles into the air. The sand dust travels through the trade winds and lands on the Caribbean coral reefs. This dust brings with it an increase in nitrogen and phosphorous; it also brings aspergillus fungi. Both are deadly to the coral reefs, causing their destruction. The increase in nitrogen and phosphorus causes algae to grow over the coral reefs, blocking sunlight and oxygen. The fungus infects the coral reefs. In studying this biome, students can develop a *cause-and-effect* chain, such as the one in Figure 3.3.

As students explore *cause-and-effect* chains, they can then predict future consequences. The death of the coral reefs would cause the fishing and tourism industries to suffer, both of which are significant contributors to the economies of the Caribbean nations (see Figure 3.4).

Figure 3.2

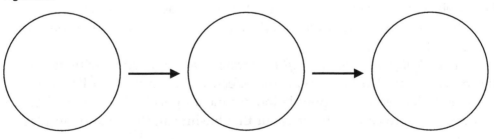

Figure 3.3

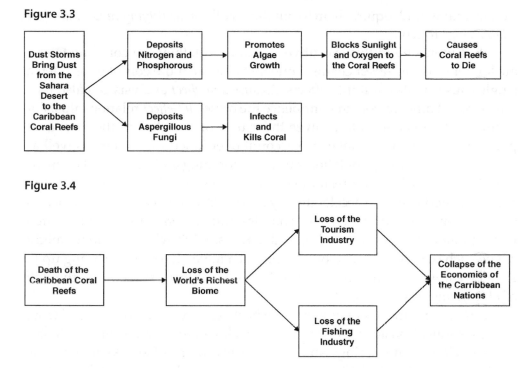

Figure 3.4

As you encounter *cause-and-effect* relationships in your content, make your thinking transparent to your students. Deliberately point out *cause-and-effect* relationships and how you identified them so that students build the executive function skill of identifying them independently.

In reading, writing, speaking, and listening, *cause-and-effect* relationships are often introduced through trigger words, such as: because, if, so, then, and therefore. Teaching students these words can help them in *identifying cause-and-effect* relationships.

Once students have an understanding of *cause-and-effect* relationships, they can tackle "what if?" questions in which you introduce a change to a situation and ask them to identify how the *cause-and-effect* relationship will be altered. If we know that darker colors of construction paper will absorb the heat from the sun and thus melt an ice cube, what change in effect on the melting of the ice cube will occur if we replace the black construction paper in an experiment with white? What if Dr. Seuss' character liked green eggs and steak instead of green eggs and ham? Spraying mosquitoes to combat the Zika virus has resulted in the death of millions of honey bees; what will happen if the honey bee becomes extinct? What if we feed ants milk? What if the Axis powers had won World War II? What would be the effect on our trip if the price of gas rose by $1 a gallon? The list could go on! When you consider your content, determine the "what if?" questions your students could pursue that would require them to put their skills of *identifying cause-and-effect relationships* to work.

As students build this executive function skill, they can continue to create longer *cause-and-effect* chains. Longer chains are more complex, as often a single cause creates multiple effects. A *cause-and-effect* analysis can also take into account other factors that influence the *cause-and-effect* relationships. For example, if you attempt to analyze the causes of a decline in the local deer population, you have to take into account deer killed by hunters as well as speculate on the deer population's need for foraging and the impact on over-population, which would result in deaths from starvation. The reduction in available food could be accelerated by deforestation caused by construction of new homes in an area. These complex interactions are best illustrated using more complex *cause-and-effect* diagrams. High school students might create such diagrams to map out the plot of a novel, the events leading up to a war, weather patterns, and so forth. The key is to focus students on the skill of *identifying causes and effects*.

In mathematical modeling, spreadsheets can be used to answer "what if?" questions. Consider the year-long Snack Fair simulation in which students decide upon offerings and build an inventory of snacks to sell. The teacher informs the students of weekly sales and students update their financials and make decisions about pricing and inventory to maximize profit. Students develop a spreadsheet (see Table 3.4) using formulas to calculate totals. Note, for example, the formula (top left of image) for calculating percentage of markup (cell E3). It is profit divided by cost. Now as the student enters price changes, the percentage of markup will be automatically calculated. Students must consider how to arrive at all calculations and enter the correct formulas. After the initial spreadsheet setup, they can engage in "what if?" analysis.

Students analyze predicted vs. actual sales and then make decisions for future weeks for pricing and quantities on hand. A student, might, for example, decide to significantly drop the price of an item to increase sales. The bottom-line change in profit will be automatically calculated (see Table 3.5), allowing students to predict the effects of their decisions.

Spreadsheets are powerful tools for engaging students in *identifying cause-and-effect relationships* and using those to make decisions. They can be used to track data in many subjects, including, most notably, math, social studies, science, and physical education.

In a STEM design process (discussed further in Chapter 6), the goal is to create a solution, that does not yet exist, to an open-ended problem. While students will engage in *cause-and-effect* thinking, it is important to prompt them to take their thinking to another level: unintended consequences.

Table 3.4

| f(x) | =D3/B3 | | | | | | | |

	A	B	C	D	E	F	G	H	I
1	Snack Fair								
2		Wholesale Price	Price You Charge	Gross Profit	% Markup	Qty On Hand	Inventory Cost	Potential Revenue	Pot. Gross Profit
3	Raisins	$0.20	$0.50	$0.30	150%	50	$10.00	$25.00	$15.00
4	Carrot Sticks	$0.30	$0.50	$0.20	67%	20	$6.00	$10.00	$4.00
5	Dried Apples	$0.30	$0.60	$0.30	100%	25	$7.50	$15.00	$7.50
6	Popcorn	$0.35	$0.75	$0.40	114%	40	$14.00	$30.00	$16.00
7	Cheese Crackers	$0.25	$0.40	$0.15	60%	30	$7.50	$12.00	$4.50
8	Juice Box	$0.40	$0.75	$0.35	88%	40	$16.00	$30.00	$14.00
9	Soy Milk	$0.75	$1.25	$0.50	67%	20	$15.00	$25.00	$10.00
10							$76.00	$147.00	$71.00
11									

Table 3.5

fx | = sum(I3:I9)

	A	B	C	D	E	F	G	H	I
		Wholesale Price	Price You Charge	Gross Profit	% Markup	Qty On Hand	Inventory Cost	Potential Revenue	Pot. Gross Profit
1	Snack Fair								
2									
3	Raisins	$0.20	$0.50	$0.30	150%	50	$10.00	$25.00	$15.00
4	Carrot Sticks	$0.30	$0.50	$0.20	67%	20	$6.00	$10.00	$4.00
5	Dried Apples	$0.30	$0.60	$0.30	100%	25	$7.50	$15.00	$7.50
6	Popcorn	$0.35	$0.75	$0.40	114%	40	$14.00	$30.00	$16.00
7	Cheese Crackers	$0.25	$0.40	$0.15	60%	30	$7.50	$12.00	$4.50
8	Juice Box	$0.40	$0.75	$0.35	88%	40	$16.00	$30.00	$14.00
9	Soy Milk	$0.75	$1.25	$0.50	67%	20	$15.00	$25.00	$10.00
10							$76.00	$147.00	$71.00

"What negative *cause-and-effect* relationship might I be creating?" Clearly the gasoline engine transformed daily life; however, the consequence was significant air pollution.

Engaging Students in Pretend and Role Play

Unstructured interaction with props and others, in which the student can take on other personas and creatively explore, build the executive function skills to enhance engagement. While you may call it by different names at different levels, play is a critical venue for building executive function and should not be overlooked.

For young students, a play kitchen, store, or workbench provides valuable opportunities for students to act out situations that build the executive function skills for engagement while fostering language skills and math skills. For older students, unstructured role playing, not in front of the class, but off on their own in pairs or small groups, will strengthen executive function skills. Have them develop a new ending to a fictional story by acting out the roles, write a fictional play where they record and act out the roles; frame it as "Free Think" time to invent a scenario, "Life Outside School" time to role play real-world scenarios, "Did You Watch That?" time where students reenact a reality television show episode with a different pathway, and so forth. While you should build in the use of content being learned, it's important to make these play moments free from assessment and critique; they should be designed to allow the student to explore for a subsequent assignment.

When students have unstructured time to invent their own interactions, they must *initiate tasks*. You might hear a young student say, "Let's put away the groceries now" and an older student say, "We are going to attempt to land on planet Camuson." In both cases, students have chosen to take on a task that will require subsequent action and possible challenges. Given it's a creative play role that they have defined, the chances are they will see it through and *persist in the task*. Few children give up on pretend play unless they're playing with someone else with whom they are having conflict. In class, you can have students play with others or also alone, in which case they will invent pretend others, and may even take on the various roles.

In order to build their play scenario, students will use many executive function skills beyond those for conscious control, moving them to build skills for engagement. As students put away the groceries, they will have to work on *identifying same and different* in order to ensure the meats go in the refrigerator while the canned goods go in the cabinet. As students navigate a spaceship, they will have to identify the good ships and beings from the bad ones, most likely explaining to their fellow space travelers how they know.

As both students play out their scenarios, they will be *thinking about multiple concepts simultaneously, identifying cause-and-effect relationships, categorizing information*, and *following multiple steps.*

As students enter intermediate grades, you may not be as inclined to offer play time, considering all the academic content you feel pressured to cover. Consider connecting the two. For example, if you see students in play working through a difficult situation, later, during academic studies that are particularly challenging, draw on that experience. "When you created your science fiction scenario, you encountered a lot of challenges landing on Camuson. What caused you to continue on and not give up?" You can allow students to engage in unstructured play and then ask them what types of scenarios they encountered that might help them in school, offering them examples such as encountering problems, meeting with success, needing to find information, being resourceful, needing others, etc. Whatever your grade level or subject area, find a way to build in unstructured, creative pretend play or role playing.

Problem-Based Learning: The Engagement Game-Changer

You probably have heard the terms project- and problem-based learning, and, sometimes, they are used interchangeably. In this book, problem-based learning refers to offering students a challenge that is open-ended (no one right answer) and authentic (believable in real life, a fantasy scenario, or science fiction.) While the term "project" can sometimes refer to closed-ended tasks, such as drawing a map or following directions to construct a model, in problem-based learning, as used in this book, the challenge is more about applying learning to a new situation.

First, you consider what authentic or real-world situation students would be able to address if they understood all the unit's content; then you present this challenge at the start of the unit to create a "felt need" to learn (Sulla, 2011). Primary students might create a personal exercise plan, allowing them to learn about parts of the body and the importance of exercise; they will read, write, and use math to generate graphs and calculate results. Intermediate students might design a plan for selling pizza slices in a variety of sizes, working to add fractions to build various interesting menu combinations, then presenting the menu ideas to a local pizzeria. Middle school social studies students might develop a plan to counter an invasive species that is disturbing the local ecosystem. High school students might consider the messages of transcendentalism that exist in music today, based on a study of the works of Thoreau and Emerson, and develop their own message for society using a media form of their choice. These are just some ideas for offering students a challenge at the launch of a unit of study to drive them into the curriculum and engage them in learning. Technology has expanded the available classroom content significantly, allowing students access to real-time information around the world. It is a powerful partner in pursuing problem-based learning.

At the early stages, you design the problems. As students progress in their ability to tackle these Authentic Learning Units (ALUs), you can offer them some creative license in aspects such as specific problem focus, audience, and how they will present information. For example, if high school students are using Metcalfe's law and geometry to analyze the strength of social networks, they can decide on the organization or company whose networks they will analyze and how they will present their recommendations. If primary students are working to educate people as to the importance of butterflies and the danger of extinction, they can make some decisions as to how they will share their information. If intermediate students are developing emergency plans for severe weather, they can make decisions as to what area of the country to address, what type of weather to address, and how they will share their plan and survival tips.

As students build their skills in developing solutions for ALUs, teachers can offer them an area of study and allow the students to design the problems. In his book, *Drive* (2011), Daniel Pink identifies three motivators that drive people's thoughts and actions: purpose, mastery, and autonomy. When students are intrigued by a problem (purpose), and believe they have the path and support to build the skills they need to provide a solution (mastery), and have some control over how and when they will learn (autonomy), they will be engaged. While this level of engagement through problem-based learning is the subject of my book, *Students Taking Charge* (Sulla, 2011), my intent here is to introduce the concept rather than cover it in depth.

As an example, in one of my former teaching roles, I taught Pascal programming to high school students. I began the course by having them play computer-based adventure games. It was a time before computer graphics were used, so everything was described in text. You'd begin by reading an introduction about perhaps stumbling upon a deserted house and deciding to go inside and take a peek. "The door slams shut and locks behind you. You must find the key to get out!" The user would then offer commands to move the player in the direction of N, S, E, or W; limited commands such as S(lide) and T(ake) allowed the user to find and collect objects that would lead to finding the key to open the locked door. Some objects helped you navigate, such as a flashlight; others helped you destroy obstacles, such as a hammer; others helped you manage your objects, such as a bag. I told my students they were going to write their own adventure games and told them to spend a couple of days playing existing games and thinking about their ideas. The content of their games was up to them; they could be as creative as they wanted. They were very excited and began working on their story-boards: characters, setting, plot, items, and exit plan. I then taught them the first Pascal command of how to place text on the screen. As they realized they needed more commands, I made the learning available to them. The results were some pretty amazing games and very engaged students. They were not just watching me introduce a Pascal command and then practicing on some contrived problem; they were building a felt need to learn program-ming language commands while creating their own scenarios and learning the skills as they needed them. My job was to develop project requirements that ensured that they learned all the commands covered in the unit; how and when they learned them depended on their felt need. The more they "played" with their ideas, the more they needed to learn, the more skills they built, and the more engaged they were. Consider how, in tackling a challenge as this, they had to *categorize* items the player could take in terms of their potential uses; they had to consider many *cause-and-effect* relationships; they had to *persist in a task*, even when they had trouble figuring out what com-mand to use next; they had to *think about multiple concepts simultaneously* as they considered the impact of a player's move on the collection of objects, location in the house, setting, and end goal. As they worked, they further solidified the executive function skills for engagement.

Consider two classrooms: In both, students have choices as to when and how they learn, working from an activity list of assignments. Some students are working independently, some in pairs, some in groups, some with the teacher. In one of the classrooms, the activities are curricular assignments aimed at content mastery as laid out by the curriculum. In the other, the activ-ities emanate from an overarching problem-based task that drives students into the curriculum. In the first, students are engaging in a variety of activi-ties to calculate perimeter and area. In the second, students are designing their dream house and thus, engaging in activities to learn to calculate perim-eter and area because of a "felt need" to learn in order to design the house. Enter the classrooms and you will feel the significant difference in energy that exists between the first, where students compliantly work through activ-ity lists, and the second, where students are engaged in learning, turning to the activities as a means to an end. Problem-based learning can make the dif-ference in engagement, encompassing all the other activities presented here.

Structures

Consider again the executive function skills that support engagement, pre-sented earlier in the chapter. You can strengthen these skills through a variety of structures built into the learning environment, regardless of content. These structures will support students' ability to engage, building the necessary executive function skills.

Task Persistence Card

Engagement requires the ability to *initiate a task* and *persist in a task*; students who give up on tasks or abruptly quit may lack the ability to *persist in a task*. A Task Persistence Card (Table 3.6) focuses students on this skill. When students want to give up, they stop and take a breath, check off how they feel, consider why they feel that way, and then make a commitment to try to persist.

The first step is to get students to recognize that they gave up on something or moved on to something else. The next step is to have them reflect on it and make a plan to stick with it. Students can have Task Persistence Cards available to take and fill out when they want to give up.

At first, you may need to initiate the use, when you notice a student giving up. You might fill it out with a student, but over time, students will come to fill them out on their own. It can be more meaningful to pair the cards with a later discussion with the teacher or a peer to share situations and how students overcame the desire to quit. Eventually, students should internalize the recognition of wanting to give up and build the willpower to *persist in the task*.

If … Then Card

Students who have difficulty *persisting in a task* may have weaknesses in attention or behavior. The If … Then Card (Table 3.7) goes beyond the reflection of the Task Persistence Card (Table 3.6) to have a student plan how to eliminate distractions.

Whereas the Task Persistence Card is used in the moment to reflect on an interrupted task, the "If … Then" card is used in advance of starting a

Table 3.6 Task Persistence Card

I want to give up on _____

I feel	Because	But I Will Try To…
❏ Frustrated		
❏ Angry		
❏ Confused		
❏ Lost		
❏ _____		

© IDE Corp., 2010–2016.

Table 3.7 If … Then Card for Taking Charge of Your Own Learning

My behavior goal: _____

_____

1) What could happen that would make you fail at your goal? Write that down under **If …**
2) If that happens, what could you do to keep working towards your goal? Write that down under **Then I Will …**
3) Go to work. Answer #4 when you're done!
4) How successful were you at remaining on task and working towards your goal? Write that down under **How Did I Do Today?**

If …	Then I Will …	How Did I Do Today?

© IDE Corp, 2011–2016.

task to consider what might cause the student to fall short of *persisting in the task*. This can be useful for helping students anticipate behavioral distractions and decide, in advance, what to do to stay focused. For example, what will students do if another student walks by and bumps into them? What if someone starts talking about something outside of the school work? Armed with these *cause-and-effect relationships*, the goal is for the student to remain productive. After the task is completed, ask students to reflect on what, if anything, happened to interrupt the task and how they handled it.

Graphic Organizers

Many of the executive function skills listed in Appendix A can be supported using graphic organizers. The circle diagrams presented earlier in the chapter for the skills of *categorization* and *cause-and-effect relationships* are examples of graphic organizers. Having a sheet with circles, boxes, or some other graphics through which they can organize their thoughts can help students visually see what is more abstract. The concrete representation of executive function skills can be a useful structure for many students, helping to focus the content and engage students in thinking through specific aspects of the content.

The well-known Venn Diagram can be used to help students focus on *identifying same and different* beyond the level of simple sorting. Have students consider two items or ideas to see how they are alike (write in outside of circle) and different (write in inside of circles). Figure 3.5 is an example of *identifying same and different* characteristics of water and hydrogen peroxide, in a beginning chemistry unit.

Note that students would have to identify, for example, that water and hydrogen peroxide are different in that water has one oxygen atom and hydrogen peroxide has two; they are similar in that they are both clear liquids.

Students at all grade levels and in all subjects could use Venn diagrams to think through similarities and differences among theories, people, concepts, and items.

For a more advanced level of thinking, once students master the two-circle Venn Diagram, use three circles (see Figure 3.6).

Young students could explore living things by comparing and contrasting, for example, a dog, fish, and frog. They would consider if they live in similar or different environments, have similar or different features, eat similar or different foods, etc. Students would employ a number of executive function skills to complete a three-circle graphic organizer.

A table graphic organizer can help students in *thinking about multiple concepts simultaneously*. In the book *Charlotte's Web*, upon learning of the impending slaughtering of Wilbur the pig, Charlotte the spider spins words about the pig into her web in the barn, such as, "Some Pig!" Her handiwork saves Wilbur's life and, instead of becoming dinner, he becomes a celebrated and prized pig. Later in the story, Charlotte is nearing the end of her life; at the fair, she lays her egg sack with her spider babies in it, and she dies. Wilbur carries the egg sack back to the barn and watches over it until her babies

Figure 3.5

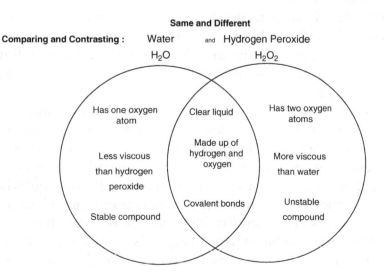

Same and Different

Comparing and Contrasting :   Water   and   Hydrogen Peroxide
H_2O H_2O_2

Has one oxygen atom

Less viscous than hydrogen peroxide

Stable compound

Clear liquid

Made up of hydrogen and oxygen

Covalent bonds

Has two oxygen atoms

More viscous than water

Unstable compound

Figure 3.6

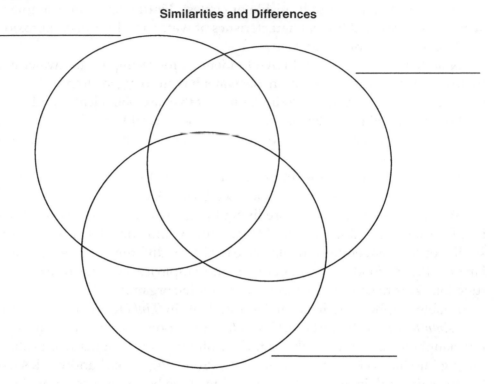

Similarities and Differences

hatch. One of the themes of the book is thinking and caring beyond one's self to others and a greater cause. Table 3.8 offers one possible graphic organizer for having students consider the events of the book as metaphorical to life, moving between the book characters and themselves and other world figures or people they know.

As introduced earlier related to *identifying cause-and-effect relationships*, if you place an ice cube on black paper and another on white paper, and put them both in the sunlight, the ice cube on the black paper will melt more quickly. Let's consider the multiple concepts at work using the graphic organizer in Figure 3.7.

In this case, the result is placed in the bottom cloud shape. The boxes with arrows are contributing factors (the graphic organizer could have many such boxes with arrows.) The student must decide what is at work here to produce the result. Just identifying the sun's heat is not enough, because both ice cubes are in the sun's heat and yet one melts more quickly. The student must consider a second concept, that of absorption of heat by different colored papers. Once the student identifies the two variables, they can see the bigger picture of what is happening. This graphic organizer focuses on *thinking about multiple concepts simultaneously* through a science experiment

Table 3.8

How does Charlotte think beyond her own wants and needs to helping others? *(enter notes and page #s)*	
How does Wilbur think beyond his own wants and needs to helping others? *(enter notes and page #s)*	
Who else in the world thinks or thought beyond his/her own wants and needs to helping others? *(include source, where possible)*	
How do you think beyond your own wants and needs to helping others? *(give examples)*	

Figure 3.7

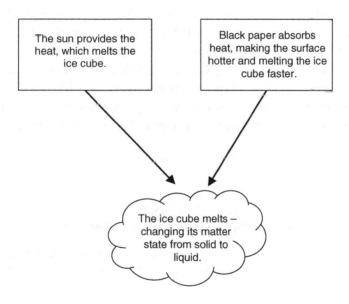

that has multiple variables at work. Graphic organizers help students make sense of content information while building executive function.

Direction Sheets

Think of an instructional activity that requires a set of procedural steps. It might be buddy reading, a Socratic seminar, a math manipulatives activity, separating an egg to use the whites in a recipe, a two-person conversation in Mandarin, or working as a group on a Google Doc or a Microsoft Office

365 document to share design ideas. Often, in a classroom, the teacher will simply walk students through the steps as a group or offer minimal direction to get students started. A better way to build the executive function skill of *following multiple steps* while accomplishing your curricular goal is to provide a printed Direction Sheet containing the steps for students to follow. While it will take some time to develop the Direction Sheet, you will have it for the future and be able to reduce the amount of class time you spend walking students through directions when they can follow on their own. Plus, you will be happy to find that your students start reading directions!

Suppose a group of students is working on a solution to an open-ended design problem. Table 3.9 offers them a set of steps to create a Google Doc through which to share their ideas with the class in order to obtain feedback.

Note that this simply represents the directions to an activity. Completing the design process and using a Google Doc are specific content skills that are presumed to be within the students' current knowledge. This is not intended to be a How-To Sheet for learning content; that will be a structure discussed in Chapter 5. This Direction Sheet makes it clear that this activity requires a series of steps. Provide each student with a Direction Sheet to follow each step, one at a time, checking off completed steps.

In my book, *Students Taking Charge* (2011), I reference a buddy-reading checklist (Figure 3.8). This set of directions allows students to take responsibility for their own actions. With very young students and those significantly lacking executive function skills, you will have to introduce them to the

Table 3.9

STEAM Design: Ideate
Generating Your Google Doc Collaboration

Now that you have engaged in the formulate, explore, and ideate stages of the design process, it's time to gather feedback from those outside your group. You'll accomplish this using a Google Doc.

☐ 1. Find all members of your team.

☐ 2. Decide where you will meet to set up the Google Doc.

☐ 3. Have each member get his or her computer and Design Notebook and meet at the specified location.

☐ 4. Which team member's last name begins with the letter of the alphabet closest to A?

☐ 5. That team member will be the starting writer.

☐ 6. **Starting Writer:** Start a new Google Doc.

☐ 7. **Starting Writer:** Change the sharing so that anyone with the link can edit.

Figure 3.8

Buddy-Reading Checklist

- [ ] Get your reading book
- [ ] Find your buddy
- [ ] Find a quiet, empty spot to read
- [ ] Sit down knee to knee
- [ ] Open your books
- [ ] Decide who will read first
- [ ] Read one page while the buddy follows along
- [ ] Switch roles
- [ ] Read for at least 10 minutes

Direction Sheet, walking them through it until they can use it on their own. You can also design it with illustrations to represent the various steps. First or second graders with reading skills should be able to follow this on their own, checking off each action as they complete it. (A laminated paper with a grease pencil for repeated use will save on paper.)

Note that in the case of cooperative learning, sometimes teachers offer a single Direction Sheet for the group so that students must pay attention to the one reading the directions. For strengthening executive function, it is important for each student to have a Direction Sheet, ensuring that the students see the directions to work toward building the skill of *following multiple steps*. As students meet with success in following Direction Sheets, deliberately reduce the number of Direction Sheets to one per group to strengthen students' executive function skills for both conscious control and engagement.

Direction Sheets can be used for individuals, pairs, and groups; they can be housed in a Resource Area (see Chapter 5). Note that each step typically represents one action. In Table 3.9, direction #3 represents multiple actions because the group members are departing from the Direction Sheet to retrieve items and return. (If you have students with significantly low executive function, you may need a card with that item broken down into three steps that they can carry with them.) Consider the procedural actions you expect students to take throughout the day or school year (hanging up coats, lining up for art class, conducting an experiment, cleaning up after an art project, setting up a writing folder, etc.). Design Direction Sheets for these various processes to build greater student engagement in their own learning and, thus, executive function skills. For students who have difficulty *following multiple steps*, hold a

Small-Group Mini-Lesson and walk them through each printed direction, helping them learn to follow the sheet rather than just following your verbal directions.

Summary for Moving from Compliance to Engagement (#EF_Engagement)

Compliant students may be appreciated by teachers, but they will not be the world's learners, thinkers, and solution finders. True learning requires engagement: grappling with content and ideas. Consider the executive function skills required and built by students' development of engagement and see how you can include activities and structures to support their growth in this area.

Executive Function Skills:

+ Identifying same and different
+ Following multiple steps
+ Identifying cause-and-effect relationships
+ Categorizing information
+ Changing perspective
+ Thinking about multiple concepts simultaneously
+ Initiating a task
+ Persisting in a task

Activities:

+ Focusing on Perspectives
+ Fostering Categorization Skills
+ Building the Concept of Cause-and-Effect Relationships
+ Engaging Students in Pretend and Role Play
+ Problem-Based Learning: The Engagement Game Changer

Structures:

+ Task Persistence Card
+ If … Then Card
+ Graphic Organizers
+ Direction Sheets.

References

Murgatroyd, S. (2011). *Rethinking education: Learning in the new renaissance*. Edmonton, AB: FuturePress.

Murphy, Paul, A. "Your Brain on Fiction," *New York Times*, March 17, 2012.

Numeroff, L. J. (2005). *If you give a mouse a cookie*. New York: Geringer.

Pink, D. (2011). *Drive: The surprising truth about what motivates people*. New York: Riverhead.

Student engagement (2016, February 2nd). In S. Abbott (Ed.), The glossary of education reform. Retrieved from http://edglossary.org/student-engagement

Sulla, N. (2011). *Students taking charge: Inside the Learner-Active, Technology-Infused Classroom*. New York: Routledge.

4

Mastering the Art of Collaboration (#EF_Collaboration)

Learning is social; we all like to learn from our peers. I observed teens in a nearby skateboarding park. They watched one another, demonstrated tricks and strategies, coached one another, challenged one another, encouraged one another, and had a great time learning. Students gravitate toward situations in which they learn with and from one another. Infants watch their parents and siblings, but as they build independence, they turn to their peers. Not only do they learn from one another, but they invent together, exercising creativity. Conventional schooling challenges that natural inclination by asking students to sit quietly in rows and work independently. As learning environments are shifting to engage students more in working in groups, students have opportunities to build productive, collaborative skills.

Collaboration involves engaging with others and others' ideas; it is a process of give and take, and, as one collective mind, taking ideas and innovations to the next level. Effective collaboration, however, does not mean "divide and conquer," with individual students tackling different aspects of a project. The key to powerful collaboration is creating situations in which students develop individual content mastery and bring that knowledge to the group to solve problems and innovate. A group of students looking to design a habitat that could accommodate a cloned dinosaur will first need to understand dinosaurs and their natural habitats. Then they can brainstorm, challenge, analyze, and create the solution. A group of students looking to develop a social media campaign to raise awareness of human trafficking must individually understand the history of human slavery, current laws, and the current reality of human trafficking. Only then can they convene to share ideas and solve the problem.

In a problem-solving environment, pairs and small groups will most likely arrive at a better solution than any one individual can; however, that depends on the competence level and communication skills of the people involved. "Two heads may be better than one, but only when we can competently discuss our different perspectives" (Kanai & Banissy, 2010). As students advance in their executive function, they gain the competence and communication skills to be a powerful collaborators. In a global economy that values collaboration, design, and invention, these are important skills. The executive function skills that are particularly critical to collaboration are (see also Figure 4.1.):

◆ Seeing multiple sides to a situation (Cognitive Flexibility)
◆ Being open to others' points of view (Cognitive Flexibility)
◆ Maintaining social appropriateness (Inhibitory Control)
◆ Overcoming temptation (Self Awareness).

Activities

As you engage students in collaborative activities, take care to structure them well so that students build the executive function skills necessary for

Figure 4.1 Executive Function Skills Related to Collaboration

Cognitive Flexibility	Shifting focus from one event to another	*Inhibitory Control*	Attending to a person or activity
	Changing perspective		Focusing
	Seeing multiple sides of a situation		Concentrating
			Thinking before acting
	Being open to others' points of view		Initiating a task
			Persisting in a task
	Being creative		**Maintaining social appropriateness**
	Catching and correcting errors		
	Thinking about multiple concepts simultaneously		
		Self-Awareness	Self-assessing
			Overcoming temptation
			Monitoring performance
			Reflecting on goals
			Managing conflicting thoughts

successful learning and application. Following are some activities for you to consider.

Discussions

Successful communication is a foundational skill for collaboration. Communication focuses on presenting "the known" clearly, concisely, and accurately. Collaboration focuses on joining with one or more others to invent "the unknown." In the process of collaborating, students move among communicating ideas, facts and evidence, opinions, challenges, questions, disagreement, and agreement. Preparing students for successful collaboration, therefore, begins with helping students build successful communication skills. As the first step toward collaboration, discussion skills allow students to apply the executive function skills they learned for conscious control and engagement.

Students build discussion skills by engaging in discussions more than by listening to someone teach them about discussion skills. Any related instructional lessons should be short and supported by checklists, graphic organizers, and protocols to scaffold learning. A student's day should be filled with opportunities to engage in structured discussions with others, including through pairs work, group work, and small-group discussions. By structured, I mean that students should have expectations for the skills they need to build during discussions so they can *set goals* and work to achieve them. For example, young students might begin with the goal of listening to others and making a statement that relates to what the last person said. Older students might focus on asking one another higher order questions to challenge thinking.

Keep whole-class discussions to a minimum because students have minimal time to speak when in a whole-class venue, and often the communication is more of a collection of student-to-teacher responses rather than a true discussion. If you fear giving up the control of your involvement with a whole-class discussion, schedule three or four small-group discussions at different times so that you can sit in as desired while the rest of the class engages in other learning activities. If you provide students with clear expectations and guidelines, you'll be surprised at what they can accomplish. One concern teachers voice about the shift away from whole group discussions is that the class may miss an important insight brought up in one of the discussion groups. However, addressing that concern should not compromise the power of providing more air time to students. You can, for example, create a sharing opportunity through a digital document, class journal, or bulletin board that students later access in a follow-up assignment.

In an effort to build discussion skills, more and more schools are teaching students the strategies of Accountable Talk® from the University of Pittsburgh. (They hold the registered trademark for the term.) Teachers can locate numerous resources online on Accountable Talk to use in the classroom. The idea is that students must be accountable in their verbal communication in three areas:

◆ Accountable to the Learning Community—Students need opportunities and instruction to learn to speak loudly and clearly so all can hear, attend to a speaker and work to understand what is being said so they can react and respond, summarize, paraphrase, ask for clarification, build on another's conversation, and respectfully disagree. The executive function skills related to collaboration that are fostered at this level are *maintaining social appropriateness*, and *overcoming temptation*.

◆ Accountable to Accurate Knowledge—Students need opportunities and instruction to learn to be specific and clear in presenting information and ideas, ensure that the information they present is factual, identify reliable resources, connect information to other information presented, and question statements made by others to ensure accuracy. Students build the executive function skill of *seeing multiple sides to a situation* as they take a comprehensive look at a topic.

◆ Accountable to Rigorous Thinking—Students need opportunities and instruction to learn to synthesize information, provide evidence for claims, build arguments through logically ordered reasons, defend positions, challenge one another, and apply higher-order reasoning to a line of thought. Students build the executive function skills of *seeing multiple sides to a situation* and *being open to others' points of views* as they consider all the facts and opinions surrounding a topic.

Keeping these three areas in mind, you can create a variety of tools to help students build communication skills that lie at the heart of collaboration. At a starting level of being accountable to the learning community, guide students to share their thoughts after reading fictional or informational text by having one student share an opinion from the reading and having the other say either "I agree because _____" or "I respectfully disagree because _____."

As students build skills, offer guiding/reflection checklists for being accountable to the learning community, such as the one in Table 4.1.

This can serve as a guide for students to read before engaging in a conversation, or it can be a reflection checklist after participation, in which case tracking the date of the reflection can help students celebrate their growth. Craft the list, depending on the grade level and developmental level for executive function skills of the students. For example, for kindergarten students, the list might look like the one in Table 4.2.

As students build skills, replace them with other, more advanced skills. For secondary students and those with well-developed executive function, hone in more so on each of the ways students demonstrate accountability to the learning community. For example, Table 4.3 offers four aspects of this area of accountability.

Table 4.1

I Am Accountable to the Learning Community
Name _____ Date _____
❑ I listen to others speaking and think about what they are saying.
❑ I contribute to the conversation in meaningful ways.
❑ I speak clearly and loud enough so that others can hear me.
❑ When I'm not sure I understand a speaker's point, I ask the speaker to clarify.
❑ I paraphrase what another speaker said in order to build on it.
❑ My points make sense based on what speaker's before me have said.
❑ I summarize the past discussion to make a related point.
❑ When I agree with a speaker, I explain why, citing the text where possible.
❑ When I disagree with a speaker, I explain why, citing the text where possible.
❑ When I introduce a new line of discussion, I use a transition phrase.

Table 4.2

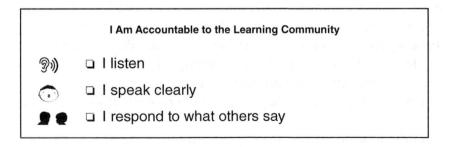

I Am Accountable to the Learning Community
❑ I listen
❑ I speak clearly
❑ I respond to what others say

Table 4.3

I Am Accountable to the Learning Community	
I Listen	**I Contribute**
❏ I listen and can empathize ❏ I listen and can paraphrase ❏ I listen and can summarize ❏ I listen for connections to what others have said and to other texts	❏ I support others' statements with facts and evidence ❏ I paraphrase and connect others' statements to mine ❏ I respectfully disagree when needed ❏ I connect mine and others' statements to the conversation and other texts
I Honor the Conversation	**I Encourage Others**
❏ I keep my comments on topic and avoid interjecting unrelated ideas ❏ If the conversation veers from topic, I offer comments to bring it back ❏ I avoid side conversations and draw the ideas into the conversation ❏ When I disagree, I do so in ways that respect those with whom I disagree	❏ I note who has not been speaking and ask for their thoughts or opinions ❏ I note if someone is having difficulty getting into the conversation and ask them for their thoughts or opinions ❏ I positively comment on those who have generated a unique insight ❏ I ask others to share more or expand upon their ideas

For students to build their skills in being accountable to accurate knowledge, focus them on substantiating their opinions, presenting facts, citing resources, and challenging questionable statements. This is a particularly important skill in the age of social media where someone can post a fabrication with such assurance that others keep reposting or retweeting until it goes viral, when it is not even accurate information. Teach students to question what they hear and read to ensure that they are maintaining accountability to accurate knowledge. For discussion guidance, offer sentence stems, such as the ones in Table 4.4.

Younger students and those with weak executive function skills can begin with simpler graphic organizers to ensure their comments are accurate, such as the one in Table 4.5.

They pick one statement they believe from their reading or information finding and must identify what pages and part of the text, or multiple texts, led them to that thought.

Secondary students should take their commitment to accurate knowledge to the next level, looking also at possible counter arguments to their ideas. If a student has a point to make, the first step is to back it up with evidence and facts. The next step is to look for arguments that run counter to the point, deciding if the point still holds up. Table 4.6 offers an example of a graphic organizer to help students in their quest for accountability to accurate knowledge.

Table 4.4

I Am Accountable to Accurate Knowledge
Holding myself accountable:
❏ I believe _____ because _____.
❏ I question _____because _____.
❏ Based on what I read, that _____, I think _____.
❏ Based on _____ , I would conclude that ____ _____.
❏ I offer you the evidence to back up my claim, found on page ___.
Holding others accountable:
❏ Can you share your evidence to support that claim?
❏ On what do you base your conclusion?
❏ What in the text led you to that interpretation?
❏ When did that happen?
❏ Where did you find that?

Table 4.5

I Am Accountable to Accurate Knowledge	
What I think:	Based on: • • • • •

Table 4.6

I Am Accountable to Accurate Knowledge		
My point:	Supported by:	Countered by:

Accountability to rigorous thinking requires more complex graphic organizers. For example, the process of synthesizing information requires students to consider multiple pieces of information and put them together in a new way to create new information. Table 4.7 offers a graphic organizer through which students consider multiple pieces of information and then develop a new idea.

I visited a classroom of students reading The City of Ember (DuPrau, 2004). I was talking with students about the possible meaning of the title. Using this graphic organizer, a student might fill it out similarly to the one in Figure 4.2.

Another aspect of accountability to rigorous thinking is that of building a logical argument. Unlike synthesis, where ideas come together to generate a new idea, a logical argument is a building of one idea on top of another. As students read, they draw conclusions based on evidence. The graphic organizer in Table 4.8 can depict the process of layering fact upon fact to arrive at a conclusion.

As students build their discussion skills, they will be strengthening myriad executive function skills that will help them in their academic pursuits. Look at Appendix A and consider how many executive function skills are in play when engaging in a discussion!

Talking builds executive function; engaging in a discussion among peers builds even more executive function. Provide students with ample opportunities to engage in discussion around content throughout the day to prepare them to engage in powerful collaborative experiences in which they are not only discussing but working to craft joint ideas and solutions.

Table 4.7

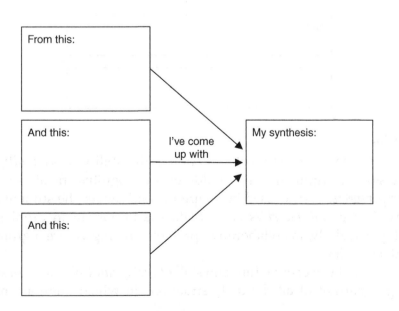

Figure 4.2

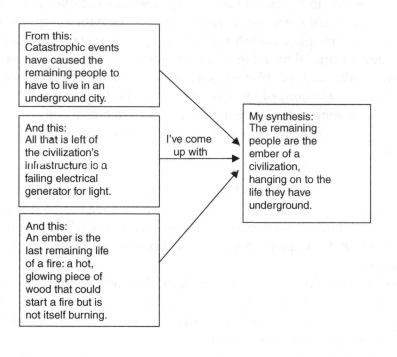

Table 4.8

If this . . .

And this . . .

And this . . .

Then . . .

Multiple Sides

A critical skill for successful collaboration is the ability to *see multiple sides* to a decision or argument. This builds on the cognitive flexibility skill of *changing perspectives*, discussed in Chapter 3, and moves the student toward empathy. *Seeing multiple sides to a situation* is important in problem solving and, particularly, in collaborative problem solving where a group must arrive at a solution.

Strengthen the executive function skill of *seeing multiple sides to a situation* by being cognizant of all the daily situations in which there are multiple sides, pausing to have students consider these different sides. A great place to start is with stories or novels. Have students consider a conflict situation in the text and determine how two or more different characters view the situation. A simple graphic organizer can help students gather their thoughts (see Figure 4.3).

A fun representation of seeing both sides of a situation is the parody book of the story of the three little pigs as told by the wolf, The True Story of the Three Little Pigs (Scieszka & Smith, 1989). Over the years, this book has

Figure 4.3 Seeing Multiple Sides to a Situation

What is happening? _____

_____

Character 1: _____

How does this character see the situation?

Character 2: _____

How does this character see the situation?

become a popular addition to school libraries, along with similar books about other fairy tales. The story, according to the three little pigs, was one of threats, bullying, and destruction by that big, bad wolf. According to the wolf, he just needed to borrow some sugar from his neighbors, the pigs, but due to his bad cold, he sneezed and destroyed their homes. While a humorous parody, it does introduce the idea that there may be *multiple sides to a situation*.

Use a similar graphic organizer for behavior and social issues in the classroom. When conflict arises between two students, have each write about how s/he sees the situation and feels about it; then have the students read one another's viewpoints to see where they agree and differ.

Students can look at many areas of content applying the executive function skill of seeing *multiple sides to a situation*. History and science are filled with such opportunities. Every historical conflict has multiple sides. Using a more complex graphic organizer, students can examine the situation from the viewpoint of several different constituencies. Figure 4.4 offers a view of the French Revolution based on four of the persons/groups involved. Students fill in the arrows with a summary of how each viewed the revolution.

Seeing *multiple sides to a situation* is also an important first step in the Design Process (covered in detail in Chapter 6). In seeking a solution to a real-world problem, the first step is to formulate the problem by identifying the ideal situation, reality, how the problem affects others, and what would

Figure 4.4

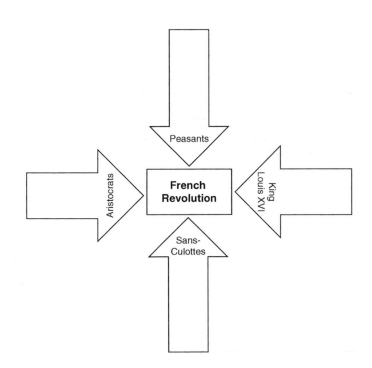

happen if the problem were not addressed. It is important for students to show empathy in this step, the ability to see a situation from another's reality. This is an executive function skill.

You Decide

To build the executive function skills that support collaboration, begin by offering a pair of students one of two choices and asking them to arrive at a joint decision. For example:

- ◆ Do you think we should eat a snack at 10:00 or at 10:30?
- ◆ Which is better for the people: democracy or socialism?
- ◆ Should the class pet be a hamster or guinea pig?
- ◆ Should the day's work begin with math or social studies?
- ◆ Should the bulletin board be lined with blue paper or yellow?
- ◆ Do you want to work at the round table or in the soft seating area?
- ◆ Should we paint the still life in water colors or acrylics?
- ◆ In the second quarter of a football game, with 50 seconds to go, on fourth down, nine yards from the goal, trailing by a score of 20 to 17, should the offense go for the touchdown or the field goal?

These two-option decisions allow the pair of students to discuss their personal points of view to see if they agree or can reach a decision. This involves discussing the possibilities, thus building the executive function skills of seeing *multiple sides to a situation* and *being open to others' points of view*. The process also builds on the executive function skills of *maintaining social appropriateness* and *overcoming temptation* when faced with frustration in the process of working toward a joint decision.

Note that by starting with pairs, the possibility of voting is eliminated, forcing students to discuss and arrive at a joint decision or deciding on a method for choosing, for example, a flip of a coin. As students mature in the process, encourage them to work to reach consensus, that is, ensuring that all involved in the decision-making either like or can live with the decision. This is a much more difficult skill than voting or randomly selecting one answer over another. From pairs, expand the group size to three, then four, then five so that students strengthen their consensus-building skills with larger groups (several tools are introduced in the structures section later in the chapter.)

The graphic organizer in Table 4.9 focuses students on three key areas of collaborative decision-making: information on which they base the answer, differences they must address, and how they arrived at a solution agreed upon by all parties.

On first use, you could remove the constraint of consensus and have the third column indicate how they arrived at their decision. You can then use that as the basis for introducing the importance of reaching consensus. The graphic organizer can be modified to fit various grade levels. For example, Table 4.10 might be used with primary level students and older students with executive function deficits, while Table 4.11 might be used with secondary students.

You can identify "You Decide" activities for any content area, including the best type of graph to use to depict information, deciding on how a character in a story or novel should react, the actions a country should take during conflict, the best approach to glazing pottery, and so forth. After stu-

Table 4.9

What is your decision?		
What information did you research to decide?	What differences did you have to address?	How did you arrive at consensus?

Table 4.10

Your Decision	Why?	How did You Decide?

Table 4.11

Points You Considered?	Counterpoints You Considered:	How You Reached Consensus:
Evidence From One Source:	Your Decision:	Evidence From Second Source:
Area of Disagreement:	Areas Requiring Further Information:	Further Information Found:

dents succeed in working toward a decision in pairs, increase the group size to three and then to four.

At this point in building collaborative skills, the focus is on simply making a decision by encouraging students to strive for consensus. Further tools for consensus-building will be introduced later in this chapter.

Synthesizing Information

Synthesis, introduced earlier in this chapter (see Table 4.7), moves collaboration to the next level, where students take existing information and put it together in new ways. This is where they move from understanding the "known" to creating the "unknown:" developing novel solutions to solving problems or creating new products or performances. Students take in information from multiple sources and, by making connections among the pieces of information, arrive at a conclusion or insight. Reading multiple accounts of a situation requires the reader to synthesize all that they read to arrive at a conclusion or insight.

At the youngest level, synthesis is best introduced through teacher discussion in small groups. Make your thinking transparent to your students. For example: "I was reading that hamsters like a lot of foods, but that you have to be careful to not have them eat too much sugar or fat. I read about some of the treats that our hamster likes. It turns out that bananas are very high in sugar, and cheese is very high in fat. Both broccoli and carrots are low in fat, but carrots have a little more sugar than broccoli. So, in thinking about all that, my synthesis is that we should only give our hamster bananas and cheese in small amounts. We can give him more broccoli with a little bit of carrots mixed in." As you present your thinking, draw or write out the different pieces of information you gathered in order to synthesize it into a decision. By walking students through the process of how you find information across multiple sources or throughout one text, and then combine the information to arrive at a conclusion, you are demonstrating how you synthesize information. You can then begin asking them to synthesize information from what they are reading.

Figure 4.5 offers a graphic organizer aimed at helping elementary students build synthesis skills.

The student gathers information on a topic and writes each piece of related information in a box. After considering all the information, the student synthesizes it into one statement, insight, or conclusion and writes it in the circle.

Table 4.12 can be used with secondary students.

Students use at least three sources from which they gather information about a topic. They summarize the most important four points made in each text. They then think through and record how each source's information connects to the others. They also consider any conflicting information or theories. Finally, they synthesize the information to develop an insight or conclusion.

Figure 4.5

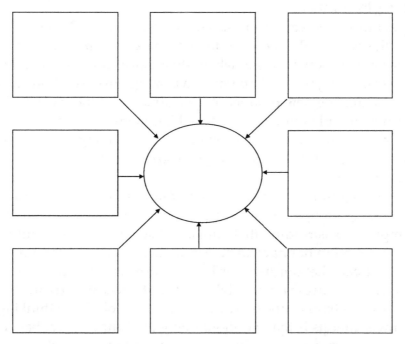

Table 4.12

Source 1:	Source 2:	Source 3:	Your Insight or Conclusion:
Top 4 points made:	Top 4 points made:	Top 4 points made:	
Connections to other sources:	Connections to other sources:	Connections to other sources:	
Conflicting Information:	Conflicting Information:	Conflicting Information:	

A popular activity for helping students synthesize in a group is the "Placemat Activity." Working with groups of four, you or the students draw a "placemat" with a rectangle or circle in the middle and the remaining area divided into three to five sections, depending on the number of students (see Figure 4.6).

Give students a central question from the content they are studying or text they are reading to solicit their ideas or opinions. Each student first spends some amount of time writing in one of the spaces, not interacting with other students in the group. After the prescribed amount of time, the group members share their thoughts and work to arrive at a synthesis of all group members' thinking. I like to think of this activity as a progression from an individual "I think" to a group "therefore." The goal is not to simply summarize, but to put all the ideas together into one, perhaps new, idea or position statement.

Brainstorming Plus

Another important skill for collaborative work is brainstorming ideas. Students in a group consider a problem to be solved or a decision to be made. Start by having students first write down their own ideas, giving them think time. Then have them start sharing ideas. It's best to go around and let each

Figure 4.6

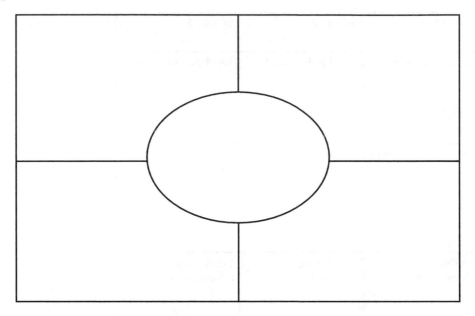

student contribute one idea or say "pass" for a round or two. Then ask for all remaining ideas. Every idea counts; no one is to react to an idea. All ideas get written down on paper. For modeling purposes, you can run the brainstorming session; however, once students understand the process, they should be able to run it on their own, perhaps with the support of a protocol, discussed later in this chapter.

After the brainstorming, students should review all the ideas to decide how well they address the issue or problem. They listen to one another share perspectives and then discuss how all involved parties will benefit from or be adversely affected by the decision, emphasizing *seeing a situation from multiple sides*. Students assign an A, B, or C (ranging from most to least favorable) for each question. A group might use a chart such as the one in Table 4.3 to capture the results, using as many rows as needed, tallying group members' opinions for each of the follow-up questions.

A modification to this process would be to have the student who brainstormed the idea first answer the three questions and decide if the idea should remain in consideration or be eliminated.

While this is only the beginning of a solution-finding process, brainstorming is an important skill. It promotes having students think and share freely, without fear of criticism. The second step begins a weeding out process. Students continue to discuss the options, applying the skills of synthesis and consensus-building.

Table 4.13

Idea	Addresses Need?			Feasible?			Interesting?		
	A	B	C	A	B	C	A	B	C

Combined Thinking

Give your class an open-ended question or a situation that requires a decision or solution. Pair up students and give them a specified amount of time to discuss as a pair. If the topic requires information searches, have students individually work on exploring the topic for a day before working together. For example, if you are simply asking an opinion question, such as, "What should the consequences be for a group member coming to group sessions without having completed the prerequisite work," you can engage students directly in the discussion. If the question requires more information, such as, "What fitness routine should we establish to warm up all our muscles before playing a sport," you will want to have students first research the topic.

When students convene, first have them discuss their ideas in pairs, working to arrive at a decision. After a specified period, have two pairs join so that four students are now engaging in a discussion of the two ideas, with the intent of arriving at a decision that all four students like. Then combine groups again for a group size of eight to discuss the two larger groups' ideas and work to arrive at a group decision. With high school students, you can expand beyond a group size of eight; otherwise, eight is probably a large enough group size for elementary students to tackle. Throughout this process, students will be strengthening the skills of *seeing multiple sides to a situation*, *being open to others' points of view*, *maintaining social appropriateness*, and *avoiding temptation* in a socially collaborative setting.

Digital Collaboration

Some say that students working on computers are not building social skills; however, the connectivity of computing devices is forcing students to build even greater social skills because they cannot always see the other person to read facial expressions and body language. Likewise, collaborating through digital venues provides students with additional opportunities to build executive function skills beyond in-person collaboration.

Years ago, B.I. (Before the Internet), I took a group of middle school students to a computer lab to write original stories. I had each student start writing, composing the story at the keyboard. After a few minutes, I told everyone to stand up and rotate one seat clockwise and continue their peer's story. I continued to do this throughout the class period. The activity required students to read what had already been written and make sense of it, and then add to the story in a way. I must have had a sense that cloud computing was coming! Now I would be able to have a group of students work on a document at the same time, commenting on and editing one another's work.

You can take advantage of cloud-based computing by having students create a document of any kind and then asking others to view and make suggested changes, allowing the original author to synthesize the suggestions. You can also have students work on the same document as they construct solutions, arguments, and ideas. Develop a new, nutritionally balanced meal for the cafeteria to serve; generate a set of rules for working in the reading corner; develop a plan for reducing the amount of electricity the school uses; create a new floorplan for arranging furniture in the classroom. Students would independently research and then join a collaborative document to offer their solutions. Out of respect for the other's work, students must exercise the executive function skills of *maintaining social appropriateness* online and *overcoming temptation*, perhaps to erase sections or delete the entire document. Through the collaborative process, they'll be building the skills of *seeing multiple sides to a situation* and *being open to others' points of view*.

Coding can be a powerful collaborative process as well, with students working to program an object, interactive game, etc. Provide guidelines that require them to discuss each step and agree upon it, rather than having one dominate while the other watches. Given that students see the results of their code immediately, they have the feedback needed to continue the conversation or change directions as they work to collaboratively solve the problem.

Structures

You can have a variety of structures in place to strengthen the executive function skills related to effective collaboration that students can draw on regularly as they engage in learning in a social environment.

Discussion Protocols

A protocol is a set of guidelines for formal interaction: rules of engagement. Whereas a Direction Sheet (Chapter 3) offers directions for completing a particular activity, and a How-To Sheet (Chapter 5) offers direct instruction in a skill, a Protocol provides students with expectations for how to engage in ongoing or repeated activities in the classroom, typically activities that involve interactions with others. You may hear the word protocol in relation to government functions in which leaders from different countries gather, following accepted rules of engagement. Your computer follows a Hypertext Transfer Protocol (http) in order to display web pages. Consider that people from all over the world create web pages and that others all over the world, on a variety of computing devices, are able to access them. That is because of the common protocol that is used by programs that generate web pages and the browsers that display them.

Given that the first step toward collaboration is the ability to discuss a topic, a key structure to support collaborative discussions are protocols. To ensure that two to eight students can meet and engage in an effective discussion, offer students clear guidelines for discussions. Start by establishing a rubric of expectations for overall performance and generate protocols for specific types of discussions. Table 4.14 offers a sample rubric of levels of powerful discussions so that students can *self-assess* and *set goals*. This can be modified to fit a specific grade or ability level.

Once you let students know your expectations for how they will behave in and contribute to a group discussion, you can use a variety of protocols to help them engage. You may already be familiar with "think-pair-share," where students first think about the topic, then pair up and exchange their thoughts, and then join a larger group to share their ideas. You may also be familiar with the "go around," where students share their thoughts one at a time. These, and other similar protocols, are good for beginning the discussion process. Table 4.15 offers a protocol for group discussions. See Appendix B for the complete set of instructions.

Table 4.16 offers a protocol for the brainstorming process discussed earlier in this chapter. For the full set of directions, see Appendix C.

You can design discussion protocols for any grade level of students and any type of discussion. The key is to offer clear steps to having an effective discussion.

Double-Entry Journal

The competent collaborator comes to the discussion table with a certain amount of expertise and ideas. The double-entry journal is a popular tool that allows students to delve into a text in advance of a conversation to gather their thoughts

Table 4.14 Levels of Powerful Discussions

	Level 1	Level 2	Level 3
Be Prepared	I brought the text.	I brought the text, my notes, and a pencil.	I brought the text, my notes, a pencil, and my mind filled with ideas about the text.
Listen	I listen to others speak without interrupting them.	I listen without interrupting to understand what others are saying.	I listen without interrupting to understand what others are saying, thinking, and feeling about the text.
Contribute	I add my comments and ideas.	I add my comments, ideas, and questions based on what others are saying.	Based on what others are saying, I add my opinions and ideas, reference the text, and ask questions that make others think.
See All Sides	I share my thoughts as to how others might feel about the information or situation.	I share thoughts and questions as to how ideas might be perceived by and affect others.	I share thoughts and questions as to how ideas might be perceived by and affect others and how we could look at a situation differently.
Synthesize	I come up with new ideas related to the information.	I connect information in the text to come up with new ideas.	I challenge myself and others to come up with new ideas by connecting information in the text through "What if?" and "How else?" questions.
Encourage Others	I ask others to share their ideas.	I notice if others aren't contributing and ask them specific questions.	I notice if others aren't contributing and ask them specific questions; I affirm others' comments.

and actions. Students fold a paper or pages in a journal in half, lengthwise. As they read, on the left they write down any sentences or phrases that are meaningful to them, including the page number for easy reference. On the right, they write down their thoughts, insights, questions, and analysis. When students come together for a discussion, they have their thoughts written in front of them, making it easier to participate in the discussion in meaningful ways. Students share their thoughts and questions, citing evidence from the text.

Consensus-Building Tools

True collaboration ends in a solution or idea arrived at by consensus. While students may tend to want to vote, voting just means the side with the greatest votes wins; it does not ensure that those on the other side can live with the decision. Collaboration must include the hard work of achieving consensus, which means everyone can at least live with the outcome. Building consensus involves discussion, presentation of opinions supported by facts, and, sometimes, arriving at a modified outcome.

Table 4.15

Group Discussion Protocol #5

Groups pose or are given questions to discuss based on texts, research, and ALU-related activities. They then follow this protocol to engage in the discussion.

1. Prior to scheduling your group discussion, ensure that each member has received a "discussion pass" from the teacher.
2. Find a place to meet, ensuring that all members can sit comfortably and hear one another.
3. Select a *TimeKeeper*, a *BirdWalk Watcher*, a *Protocol Promoter*, and a *Materials Person*.
4. Use the "Placemat Activity" to individually write down key thoughts from your notes about the question you are discussing. The *TimeKeeper* should allow 5 minutes for the group to do so.
5. Begin a discussion using the following guidelines:
   a. Everyone listens to the speaker. No one starts searching for information for their next statement until a person finishes speaking.

Table 4.16

Effective Discussions: Brainstorming Protocol

Question or Problem: _____ _____

Group Members: _____

1. You will need a *Reader*, *Recorder*, *TimeKeeper*, and *Encourager*. If you have fewer than four group members, double-up the roles as needed.
2. The *Reader* will read these directions to the group to guide the brainstorming process.
3. The *Recorder* will fill in the top two lines at the top of this page.
4. The *TimeKeeper* will keep track of the time to help keep the group on task.
5. Individually, spend 5 minutes thinking of ideas to address the question or problem. Don't judge any ideas; just keep generating.
6. The *Encourager* will go around the group, asking each person to offer one idea. No one is to comment on the ideas, positively or negatively. Keep going around; generate as many ideas as possible. The *Recorder* will write the ideas down so that everyone can see them.

When asking groups of students to make a decision, ask them to reach a consensus. An easy approach to consensus building is to ask students to express their support of a decision with thumbs up (like it), thumbs down (dislike it), or thumbs sideways (can live with it.) Those with their thumbs down should express what they don't like about the decision. Others can then clarify their positions, but the work should be in arriving at a modified decision with which everyone can live.

Edward deBono founded the Cognitive Research Trust and developed a myriad of tools for creative and critical thinking, known as the CoRT tools. One of his tools that works well in the consensus-building process is called PMI, which stands for Pluses, Minuses, and Interesting ideas or questions. When discussing a decision, most people have a preference and work to argue for their side. PMI forces group members to look at a decision from their side, the other side, and a third, generative perspective. It broadens the discussion and helps group members to consider the pros and cons of their own ideas.

To teach students the structure, give them a three-column table with P, M, and I as the column headings. Present an idea, such as the decision to close schools on Wednesdays and Sundays rather than Saturdays and Sundays. Give students 3 minutes (you may add a minute or two during initial training) to write down exactly two pluses, two minuses, and two interesting ideas or questions. You want students to address all three perspectives and not dwell on one, thus the direction to generate two, not one, not three, points for each. You want the pressure of time so that students focus on the task at hand and present their initial reactions. After the 3 minutes, have students go around and present their pluses and consider the group's responses. Then have students go around and present their minuses in the same way. Finally, have students go around and present their interesting ideas and questions. The latter usually leads to further discussion and often produces a solution that everyone likes or can live with. Once students know how to use the tool, just make stacks of the PMI charts available. You'll find that students themselves will grab them when they are stuck in working on arriving at a decision (learn more at www.cortthinking.com).

Another powerful tool from deBono for consensus building is the Six Thinking Hats, which he introduced in a book by the same title in 1985, transforming the way groups collaboratively think and arrive at decisions. As students discuss a topic, and, in the case of consensus building, a proposed solution, they look at it from six perspectives, each one represented by a colored hat:

> Red Hat—Emotion: How does this make you feel? What's your initial, gut reaction?
> Yellow Hat—Positive: What is great about this solution?
> Black Hat—Skeptic: What could go wrong with this solution? Why might it not work?
> White Hat—Facts: What other information is needed to decide?
> Green Hat—Possibilities: What other, new, ideas might you consider as a solution?

Blue Hat—Process: Have we considered all six hats and resultant ideas?

You can create a grid of the six hats as a graphic organizer to allow students to write down their ideas in advance of a conversation. During the conversation, students should use the hat names as they discuss. As they do, they will start addressing their peers with comments like, "Take off your black hat for a minute and put on your yellow hat," which replaces a comment such as, "Stop being so negative." The six hats bring a productivity atmosphere to the consensus-building conversation.

Working to build consensus challenges students to exercise all the executive function skills that support collaboration. As you prepare students to become productive citizens who solve world problems, collaboration and the related executive function skills will support them in their pursuits.

Summary for Mastering the Art of Collaboration (#EF_Collaboration)

The ability to collaborate makes someone a valuable classmate, colleague, employee, life partner, and world citizen. Consider the executive function skills required and strengthened by student development of collaboration skills. See how many activities and structures you can build into students' academic pursuits to enhance their skills toward moving beyond seeing the world only through their eyes and addressing only their needs and wants to be part of a greater, problem-solving, community.

Executive Function Skills:

- ◆ Seeing multiple sides to a situation
- ◆ Being open to others' points of view
- ◆ Maintaining social appropriateness
- ◆ Overcoming temptation

Activities:

- ◆ Discussions
- ◆ Multiple Sides
- ◆ You Decide
- ◆ Synthesizing Information

- ◆ Brainstorming Plus
- ◆ Combined Thinking.

Structures:

- ◆ Discussion Protocols
- ◆ Double-Entry Journal
- ◆ Consensus-Building Tools.

References

de Bono (1985). *Six thinking hats*. Boston, MA: Little Brown.

DuPrau, J. (2004). *The city of Ember*. New York: Yearling.

Kanai, R. & Banissy, M. J. (2010). Are two heads better than one? *Scientific American*: http://www.scientificamerican.com/article.cfm?id=are-two-heads-better-than.

Scieszka, J. & Smith, L. (1989). *The true story of the three little pigs*. New York: Viking.

5

Embracing Empowerment
(#EF_Empowerment)

There's an old adage, "Give a man a fish, and you feed him for a day; teach a man to fish and you feed him for a lifetime." The latter is empowerment: giving someone the power, in this case, through skill-building, to take control of his life.

In *Learner-Active, Technology-Infused Classrooms* (Sulla, 2011), teachers empower students to make decisions about how, when, and with whom they work. While it may be necessary to learn how to properly cite evidence from a text, teachers can provide a variety of ways for students to learn that skill, including a video, How-To Sheet, website, or Small-Group Mini-Lesson. Presenting students with expectations and options but allowing them to make decisions empowers them to take responsibility for their own learning. Based on your comfort level, you can increasingly identify ways to empower your students.

Being empowered, however, is not enough; you need some foundational skills to be able to rise to the challenge. Those executive function skills that support empowerment are listed below (see also Table 5.1):

- ◆ Catching and correcting errors (Cognitive Flexibility)
- ◆ Setting goals (Planning)
- ◆ Managing time (Planning)
- ◆ Self-assessing (Self-Awareness)
- ◆ Monitoring performance (Self-Awareness)
- ◆ Reflecting on goals (Self-Awareness).

Table 5.1 Executive Function Skills Related to Empowerment

Cognitive Flexibility	Shifting focus from one event to another	Self-Awareness	Self-assessing
	Changing perspective		Overcoming temptation
	Seeing multiple sides to a situation		**Monitoring performance**
	Being open to others' points of view		**Reflecting on goals**
	Being creative		Managing conflicting thoughts
	Catching and correcting errors		
	Thinking about multiple concepts simultaneously		
Planning	**Setting goals**		
	Managing time		
	Working towards a goal		
	Organizing actions and thoughts		
	Considering future consequences in light of current action		

Note that in order to be empowered, you must strengthen your skills of planning and self-awareness; otherwise, you'll be unable to exercise that power. The executive function skills that are critical to empowerment are best addressed through classroom structures; however, some activities can be used as well. Following is a collection of activities and structures you can use to strengthen students' executive function skills related to empowerment.

Activities

Recreating a Drawing

In this activity, one student draws an image while another attempts to recreate it by following only verbal directions. While the activity draws on many executive function skills, it focuses on the empowerment-related skills of *catching and correcting errors*, *self-assessing*, and *monitoring performance*. One student draws a simple figure made from geometric shapes (see Figure 5.1) and gives only verbal directions to a partner, who attempts to recreate the drawing using only the verbal directions. After completing the exercise, the two reflect on the accuracy of the drawing and the directions, seeking to improve their joint performance on the next round. The pair continues taking turns, seeking to continually improve their ability to give and follow the directions to replicate the drawing.

This activity may be used at any grade level. Appendix D offers a complete set of directions to use with students; modify as needed to suit the grade level or executive function strength. As students succeed in completing simple drawings, increase the complexity, including having older students

Figure 5.1

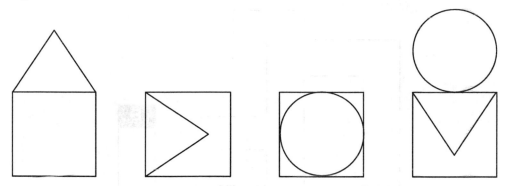

estimate lengths, describe one component as a fractional length or size of another, and estimate angle measurements.

Navigating a Maze

In this activity, students each construct a maze using labels or a textured material that a partner can navigate with an index finger and eyes closed. Students could use popsicle sticks glued to cardboard, adhesive address labels cut into strips, construction paper strips glued to paper, and so forth. The important characteristic is that the maze material is raised enough or of a different texture so that the navigating student does not get confused between the maze path and the background. At first, students should be instructed to limit the length and complexity of the maze, using a beginning sticker or marker, a designated number of steps with which to build the maze, and an ending marker (see Figure 5.2). There would be no dead ends in the maze.

As students attempt to trace the path of one another's mazes with eyes closed, using only an index finger, they will be in a continual mode of *catch-*

Figure 5.2

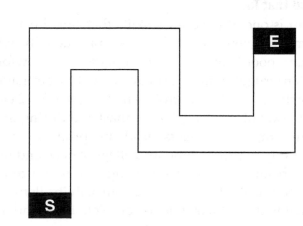

Figure 5.3

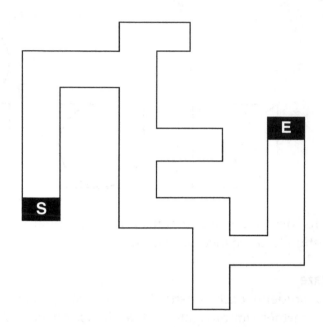

ing and correcting errors and *monitoring performance* to stay on the path. After completing a maze, students should reflect on what they learned about the maze. Students should repeat a maze several times, working to improve their speed as they practice, *monitoring their performance* and reflecting on their improvement over time.

As students build their ability to follow simple mazes, they can build more complex mazes with dead ends (see Figure 5.3). Students navigating for the first time will have to activate a lot of executive function skills to identify a successful path out. Their goal, then, through repeated practice, will be to navigate the maze quickly and accurately.

How Much Time Did That Take?

Time management is one of the critical skills that can either make or break you; poor time management can lead to poor productivity, which leads to increased stress and poor health. College students, with newfound freedom and flexibility, often struggle with time management as they navigate an environment with much less teacher control than the typical K-12 classroom. The executive function skill of *managing time*, if mastered during the K-12 school years, can not only improve students' academic productivity during those years, but significantly improve students' college, career, and life pursuits.

Managing time begins with students being able to tell time and have a sense of how much time it takes to complete an activity. Before students can schedule how they will use their time to complete tasks and achieve goals, they must build the foundational skill of *managing time*. To start strengthening this skill, help students build an awareness of activity completion and how long different activities take to complete. It might be obvious to you that it takes less time to pour a glass of water than to wash and slice an apple, and both take less time than walking a mile; but that's because you have the executive function skill to understand that.

Students do not typically master the skill of telling time until the second grade, so younger students should focus only on activity completion, further solidifying the executive function skills of *initiating* and *persisting in a task*, rather than the actual time each took. For kindergarten and first- grade students, you might create a set of images to represent various activities and have students glue the images onto a blank sheet of "Today's Activities," to track their accomplishments throughout the day. You might simply create a sheet of activities with images and have students color in a star upon completion (See Figure 5.4). The goal is to have them gain an understanding of completion of one activity and moving on to another. You could insert empty clocks that students would fill in as they begin and/or end an activity. This

Figure 5.4

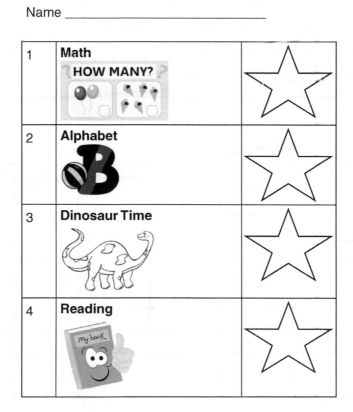

would focus them on the relationship between the clock and managing time, even though they do not yet know how to tell time.

Beginning in second grade, start the day or class period by having students write down the time. Then, as the class or individuals complete an activity, have students write it down and write the time for starting the next activity, keeping a list of accomplishments throughout the day. The list might include reviewing homework, working on an assignment, listening to a teacher's lesson, working with a partner on a project, going to lunch, etc. The goal is to have students recognize each activity as being associated with a start time (see Table 5.2).

For students who can tell time, have them record the start and end time of an activity and calculate the elapsed time (see Table 5.3).

Table 5.2

Name _____ Date _____

Start Time	Activity	Completed

Table 5.3

Name _____ Date _____

Activity	Start Time	End Time	Elapsed Time

Having students record time allows them to build a sense of how much time it takes to accomplish certain tasks. After collecting a week or more of time data, have students reflect on how much time an activity typically takes so they get a sense of how much time they need when they engage in that activity in the future. For example, if one of the activities is to write sentences from vocabulary words, students can see how much time it typically takes them to plan for the future. It is difficult for students to guess how much time has passed, as the more engaged students are, the more quickly time passes. It is, however, valuable for students to gain an understanding of how long it takes them to complete certain tasks for future scheduling and time management.

As students become familiar with the tracking process, add a column for estimated time and have them plan how much time they intend to spend on each activity. Upon completion of the collection of activities, students should reflect on their anticipated vs. actual time. Did the activity take more or less time than they thought? Would that cause them to adjust their times for future, similar activities? For activities that took longer than they thought, were they distracted or off task at all? If so, how might they reduce distractions to improve their performance in the future? Aided by these reflective questions, students will be building the executive function skills of *managing time*, *self-awareness*, *monitoring performance*, and *reflecting on goals*. These skills will, in turn, better position them to succeed when empowered to make decisions and take responsibility for their own learning.

For middle and high school students, have them use technology to additionally track how much time they spend on a particular activity across the week, perhaps creating a line graph of time spent across the week. For example, they might track how much time they spend on homework, learning activities, research, discussions, practice activities, solution generation, presentation development, and so forth. They can create a pie chart of how they spend their time in a given week, using those same activities. These are the beginning steps to improving one's productivity. For homework, students could track how they spent time outside of school to gain a greater sense of their overall time management skills. For a long-term project or paper, have students map out a plan with intermediate deadlines. Then have them track progress and note whether and why they are ahead of, on, or behind schedule.

The more teacher-directed classroom activities are, the less empowered students are and the fewer opportunities they have to build these critical executive function skills. Reflect during your lesson planning to see where you might provide students with options for managing how they will use their time. For example, if you have three activities you want to complete, and they do not have to occur in any particular order, allow students to decide the order and schedule them. If you have a skill you want to teach, consider whether or not you might offer multiple ways to learn that skill, for example, through a lesson with you, a video, a How-To Sheet, etc. Then let students plan to engage in one or more, scheduling how they will spend their time. The key is to build students' awareness of how they use time so that they can *self-assess*, *monitor performance* in relation to time, *set goals*, *reflect on goals*, and, ultimately, *manage time*.

Structures

Empowerment is not something you teach as much as something you foster through the classroom environment using a variety of structures. Following are several that will help build the executive function skills that are key to empowerment.

Resource Area

If a teacher hands out papers or other instructional resources and some students don't receive them, it's the teacher's fault. When students are empowered to gather the necessary resources they need to complete activities, when they are lacking those materials, it's their fault. While fault may sound like a strong word, the point is that for students to build a sense of empowerment, they must take responsibility for their own learning, and one of those responsibilities is acquiring the necessary materials for learning.

Create a Resource Area for students to access throughout the day or class period as needed. It could be a table, hanging folders on a wall, file boxes, a digital drive, or any other area where instructional resources can be housed to be accessible to students. If students are about to engage in a discussion, for example, they can retrieve the discussion protocol (Appendix B) from the Resource Area. Likewise, students can retrieve How-To Sheets, Direction Sheets, calculators, articles, markers, and more from the Resource Area.

If your students have adequate access to technology, many of your instructional resources can be housed online and even be digital themselves. A music teacher created a collection of videos of him demonstrating guitar chords and playing techniques for his guitar students. An art teacher created a collection of videos of art-making techniques that students can access from their smartphones. A group of kindergarten teachers created a collection of "How To" videos for students, including how to use a gluestick, draw faces, write letters, and more; students use a QR code to access the videos.

Using a Resource Area, students are empowered to access materials as they need. In a differentiated learning environment, students will be working on different activities at the same time. They will go to the Resource Area to retrieve what they need when they need it. If you are planning a whole-group lesson for which students will need a particular handout, advise students to retrieve what will be needed at some point prior to the start of the lesson. That way, instead of you handing out papers during the lesson, your students will come to the lesson with the materials they need. (Well, they won't at first, but you'll keep reinforcing this!) Note: you will want to avoid having the entire class head to the Resource Area at the same time; so, you should either let them know well in advance to be prepared for the lesson or have only one student from a group gather the materials needed for all the group members.

Anchor Charts

When you consider your content, you can probably identify several topics that could be summarized in a table, chart, or poster: a writer's checklist, elements of a story, cooking measurements, how a bill becomes a law, types of angles, plot structure, multiplication strategies, culture, economics vocabulary, warm and cool colors, scientific method, design process, and more. Anchor charts offer a quick visual for a process or definition; they anchor a student's thinking. They also empower students by providing them with a visible reference so they can access help on their own. Run a web search on anchor charts for your subject area to see what you can find.

Anchor charts should come and go on the walls (or if you like, on a digital wall on a class website), remaining visible during the time students are first learning a process, concept, or skill. Depending on the size, you can then archive them for students to access at a later date if needed. You can create anchor charts and/or you can have students create them. A fifth-grade teacher was offering a language arts lesson and a student suggested that he could make an anchor chart to make it easier to understand; and he did. So, anchor charts can empower students by providing them with key information and by inspiring them to design their own.

The Great Student Rubric

The Great Student Rubric is a powerful structure intended to focus students on behaviors, work habits, and characteristics that will help them excel academically. You might include expectations for homework completion, preparedness, noise level, staying on task, etc. You might also include characteristics, such as persistence, curiosity, and optimism. The Great Student Rubric provides students with clearly articulated expectations for behavior and work habits, focusing on executive function more than subject-area content. More than a list of rules, it offers a progressive scale of criteria towards success. It is intended to serve as a structure to which students will refer regularly to *self-assess* and jointly assess with the teacher, to *set goals* for continued growth, allowing them to take greater responsibility for themselves as learners.

This section contains three different rubrics for you to use as models. Even though one may not fit your grade level or need as is, review each and read through the descriptions, as you may identify aspects you'll want to incorporate into your own Great Student Rubric.

Introduce the Great Student Rubric you develop and have students discuss the various behaviors, *self-assess*, and *set goals*. Once students are familiar with a Great Student Rubric from prior grade levels, you can engage them in helping you design one for the class. In the case of the latter, it's a good idea to develop your desired rubric first so that you have some ideas for steering them toward desired habits.

As students use the Great Student Rubric, they identify where they fall on the rubric for each category and then work to move to the right toward greater mastery. Students should refer to the Great Student Rubric throughout the day and reflect on their performance daily.

The rubric section pictured in Table 5.4 was designed for primary level students, but could be used by intermediate students who significantly lack executive function skills. (See Appendix E for the full rubric.)

Note that the column headings represent continual growth, never failure, and the wording is all positive. For example, instead of "I don't remember to bring in my work" use "I bring in my work when reminded." The purpose of the rubric is to offer students a path to success, not to evaluate them as failing in executive function. If your students are very low in executive function, you could begin, for example, with "I bring in my work when someone at home reminds me" and then move to the student creating a reminder, then to remembering on his/her own.

Table 5.5 offers a framework for a Great Student Rubric for students from intermediate through high school; modify the language and behaviors to fit your students' specific grade levels and needs. (See Appendix F for the full rubric.)

Note that the first row addresses the concept of individual responsibility. At the early level of success, the student comes to class with homework and materials; with the teacher's prompting the student gets started. Once the student is accomplished at that level, the next level requires getting started without prompting, using a Help Board to signal a need for the teacher's assistance when stuck, and completing any activities for group work. The

Table 5.4 Great Student Rubric: Version 1

	Learning	*Practicing*	*Got it!*
I'm Ready to Learn	• I bring work, books, pencils or other tools when reminded. • I get to work when told.	• I come to class with all tools needed to learn. • I get my work done right away without being told.	All of Practicing plus I check the board for any changes or information from the teacher before getting to work.
I'm Responsible	• I complete most work on time. • I find a safe place to store my papers and other items so I don't lose them.	• I complete all my work on time. • I know where all my papers and belongings are. • I meet all deadlines.	All of Practicing plus when finished early, I spend time improving my work before handing it in.
I Pay Attention	• I usually stay on task. • I quickly get back on task with a reminder from teachers or classmates.	• I stay on task. • I quickly get back on task when distracted. • I keep off-task conversations for lunch or free time.	All of Practicing plus I take steps to stay focused, including moving to a better workspace to reduce distractions.
I Can Work with Others	• I carry out my role with reminders. • I sometimes share my materials and space.	• I work with my team to decide on roles and jobs. • I carry out my role effectively. • I share material and space.	All of Practicing plus I make sure that all group members have opportunities at all roles, materials, and classroom spaces.
I Manage My Time	• I plan my schedule with help. • I stick to my schedule with reminders. • I explain why some activities took longer or shorter.	• I plan my schedule without help. • I complete activities within the time limits. • I adjust my plan as needed while still meeting expectations.	All of Practicing plus I explain my strategies for planning and scheduling to others.

From www.ideportal.com © 2010–2015, IDE Corp.

Practitioner and Expert columns are increasingly demanding. This row reinforces executive function skills related to individual responsibility, previously introduced.

Row two focuses on the Two-Pocket Folder (described later in this chapter) used by students in the *Learner-Active, Technology Infused Classroom* (Sulla, 2011) to manage their completed and in-progress assignments. This row could be modified to match whatever assignment management tool you use, such as a work portfolio, folder, or notebook.

Table 5.5 Great Student Rubric: Version 2

	Novice	Apprentice	Practitioner	Expert *All of Practitioner plus*
Individual Responsibility	comes to class ready to learn: • brings completed homework • has materials and necessary tools • with prompting, starts tasks	• starts tasks without prompting from teacher • uses the "Help Board" rather than interrupting the teacher • completes activities for group work	• completes all work to be handed in on time when in need of help: • re-reads directions • reviews notes • quietly asks others for help • adds name to "Help Board" • if unable to continue, moves on to something else productive	When finished early, spends time improving the work to be handed in or works on challenge or optional activities
Folder Organization	• brings any current and prior work needed for class each day	• organizes work for easy access using "in progress" and "completed" pockets	• stores current schedule and activity list, direction sheets, current unfinished work, and completed work for the unit in ways that allow easy access • stores papers from previous units at home	able to explain organization strategy and changes made over time
Focus	• with prompting from teacher or peer, starts tasks • if off task, with prompting from teacher or peer, resumes task	• recognizes loss of focus and gets back on task • when working individually, chooses a seat to minimize distractions	• stays on task throughout an activity • switches from one activity to the next with minimal "down time" • refrains from distracting others • reserves off-task conversations for out-of-class time	explains strategies for effectively staying focused during school and homework
Participation	participates in group lessons and activities	• comes to group lessons and activities prepared • asks and answers questions to clarify content or directions • offers ideas	• follows through on all group responsibilities • actively listens to others and relates comments to their contributions • uses text to back up opinions • asks higher-order, content-related questions	• offers praise and constructive criticism to peers • accepts and utilizes constructive criticism

For each row, the Practitioner column represents the expected performance. The first two columns are stepping stones toward achievement and the Expert column is a reach for those who can achieve at higher levels.

In the rubric in Table 5.5, row three focuses on a specific executive function skill for conscious control: *Focus*. Each column deepens the student's understanding of *focusing* and *overcoming temptation* to lose *focus*. Row four returns to a concept. Design your Great Student Rubric to address the skills and procedures that are most important and useful to you and your students.

Table 5.6 focuses on growth mindset, a term made popular by Carol Dweck (2006), and grit, a term made popular by Angela Duckworth (2016). See Appendix G for the full rubric.

The rubric terms are inspired by the character program of the Kipp School, located in New York City. The program, based on the research of, most notably, Angela Duckworth, Carol Dweck, Chris Peterson, and Martin Seligman, focuses on building the skills of zest, grit, optimism, self-control, gratitude, social intelligence, and curiosity (learn more at www.kipp.org). These are powerful traits related to success in life; they are also strongly related to executive function. The rubric in Table 5.6 offers a design that is more about attributes than areas of responsibility.

All three rubrics offer you different options for designing your own Great Student Rubric. Design your rubric to represent a combination of concepts, structures, executive function skills, behaviors, protocols, etc. that fit your subject, grade level, and students' needs. Only use criteria that are objective and can be observed or demonstrated. Criteria such as "tries" and "understands" cannot be observed or demonstrated. Guide your word choice with the question, "What would that look like?" as you develop your criteria.

Avoid any criteria that indicates the student is unable or not achieving. The first column should represent a first step in the right direction. You would not want to indicate a negative outcome as you don't want students to aspire to that. For example, the first column might say "comes to class" rather than "is not prepared for class." In this case, showing up unprepared is the first step on the rubric. The second column might read, "comes to class with a notebook and pen." The rubric should represent a set of positive steps. If your students significantly lack executive function, you'll want to include phrases such as "with the teacher's help," "with reminders," or "with prompting."

Build on your rubric as the year progresses, offering several rows to start the year and then eliminating rows and/or adding new rows as time passes, as students build skills. The skills you are building in the beginning of the year may not be the ones on which you will focus later in the year. For example, you may establish rows for end-of-day procedures or for students' readying

Table 5.6 The Great Student Rubric: Version 3

	Novice begin reflecting here	Apprentice	Practitioner read here first	Expert all of Practitioner plus
Grit and Optimism	• sets clear goals • identifies skills and topics that are a struggle and believes growth is possible	• perseveres with even difficult tasks • when struggling, identifies reasons behind failure and tries new strategies	• consistently hands in quality work on time • persists through challenges to achieve quality work • analyzes failures and setbacks and develops strategy for breaking through	• articulates strategies to develop grit • explains how optimism affects success in class
Self-Control	• brings prior work necessary for class each day • gets to work with reminders • when off-task, returns to task when prompted	• gets to work right away without reminders • maintains appropriate volume in class • identifies at least two strategies to stay focused in class • has responses for distraction • uses directions to increase success	• uses rubric to help guide learning throughout the unit • accurately self-checks work in class • uses directions and notes to help answer questions before asking others • refrains from distracting others • refrains from interrupting others when speaking	• explains organizational strategies and changes made over time • explains the strategies used for effectively managing time in school and at home
Collaboration: Gratitude and Social Intelligence	• identifies a clear role during partner or small group work • is polite to peers (including *please* and *thank-you*) • is polite to teacher (including *please* and *thank-you*) • keeps temper in check	• adapts to different social situations • allows others to speak without interruption (actively listens) • follows through on partner or small group responsibilities • helps group meet goals • works to resolve differences with others	• able to find solutions to conflicting opinions with others • shows appreciation • puts forth effort to make a difference for others in class • makes suggestions to group to work more effectively	• assists group members in reaching consensus and resolving conflict
Curiosity and Zest	• identifies topics in class that are interesting/exciting to explore	• demonstrates enthusiasm for learning and applying content	• asks questions to aid in learning more effectively • approaches new situations with excitement and energy	• makes real world connections to content from class without prompting

This rubric was inspired by Paul Tough's book, *How Students Succeed*, and the character program at the Kipp School in NYC.

From www.ideportal.com © 2010–2015, IDE Corp.

themselves to go to their specials' classes. Once the year is underway and students achieve success in these rows, eliminate them and add others.

You can also begin with a rubric of specific work habits, as in the rubrics in Table 5.4 and 5.5, and later move to a rubric more focused on personal attributes, as in the rubric in Table 5.6. If you are working across a school, you can design a grade-level rubric to be shared by students and teachers across a grade, with each successive grade-level rubric demanding more sophisticated skills.

When you first introduce the Great Student Rubric, consider the grade level. You can allow students to read through it, assessing themselves and generating clarifying questions. For young students and those significantly lacking executive function, introduce one row of the rubric at a time, adding rows in subsequent days or weeks. This will help students *focus*, and it will prevent over-stimulation and confusion. A middle school English language arts teacher posts rubric rows around the room so that he and his students can refer to them regularly, an anchor chart of sorts.

If students begin using a Great Student Rubric in kindergarten, by middle school, they should be designing their own personalized versions, assessing their mastery of the various executive function skills and determining where to focus their efforts. By high school, you might have them address even more sophisticated skills and concepts such as productivity, empathy, balance, innovation, entrepreneurship, etc.

The Great Student Rubric is a robust structure for building executive function towards empowering students to take control of their own learning. It can address all the executive function skills related to empowerment:

◆ *Self-assessing*—At first, you may have students *self-assess* based on just one row, one skill; over time, they will focus on the entire rubric.

◆ *Monitoring performance*—In addition to learning to *self-assess*, which is a skill in the moment, focus students on *monitoring their performance* over time. Have them note how well they demonstrated the rubric criteria at the Practitioner or Expert level each day and reflect on progress over time, including *reflecting on their goals* to improve their performance.

◆ *Setting goals* and *reflecting on goals*—Have students use the Great Student Rubric to set goals for the day or week. Have them reflect regularly on their individual goals to determine how close they are to achieving them. In some cases, they may want to set a goal that's not included in the rubric; they can then design a rubric row of their own. Consider leaving a blank row at the bottom for that purpose.

◆ *Managing time* and *catching and correcting errors*—While these skills are not addressed in the use of the rubric, include a row for each on the rubric to focus students on those skills for embracing empowerment.

How-To Sheets

Janelle needs to survey her classmates as part of a math unit. She wants to create a *Google* form but doesn't know how. She walks over to the Resource Table and retrieves a How-To Sheet on creating a *Google* form. She follows each step on this three-page document and, at the end, successfully creates her survey form.

A How-To Sheet is a "learning activity," meaning it focuses on a discrete skill or concept, provides step-by-step directions to follow, and, where possible, provides feedback (Sulla, 2015). In this case, the successful completion of the form confirms achievement for the student. Appendix H offers a How-To Sheet on using a Venn diagram. Through How-To Sheets, students learn academic skills by following directions. In the process, they exercise many executive function skills, including those critical to empowerment. As they follow directions and note the outcomes of their actions, they are *catching and correcting errors*. Throughout, they *self-assess* and *monitor progress* toward the goal.

To get started creating How-To Sheets, identify those skills or concepts that you typically present in whole-class Benchmark or Small-Group Mini-Lessons. Ask yourself if some, or all, of your students might alternatively learn or practice by following a set of written directions. Write up the directions such that each numbered direction represents exactly one step in the process. Be as specific as possible. Use screenshots, images, and illustrations to offer a visual guide as well. Include warnings and ways to overcome typical mistakes. For example, in a How-To Sheet for reading a graduated cylinder, you would include a statement such as, "If you aren't eye level with the top of the liquid, your reading will not be accurate." Be sure to keep each How-To Sheet focused on one discrete skill or concept. For example, rather than one How-To Sheet on creating graphs, have one for creating bar graphs, one for creating line graphs, one for creating pie graphs, one for creating scatter plots, and so forth. As students come to understand the purpose of How-To Sheets, encourage them to create ones for others. The act of creating the How-To Sheet will empower them to contribute to the classroom collection of resources and build important executive function skills. Create a rubric or checklist to guide their design work.

Keep How-To Sheets organized in a Resource Area. You might mark the last sheet of a pile with a note to let the teacher know this How-To Sheet needs to be replenished. Laminate How-To Sheets so students can reuse them.

Ask students to wrap up an activity by reflecting on how well they could follow the How-To Sheet. This allows them to start to build a greater understanding of their learning style preferences and how they can learn through a variety of venues. Some students may say they prefer to learn directly from the teacher. This opens the door for a conversation about the similarities and differences: when it would be possible to learn from a How-To Sheet and when it might be better to learn from the teacher's lesson. For example, students who have performed well in math and have learned to factor binomial equations might use a How-To Sheet to learn to factor trinomial equations. Students who are struggling with the concept and may need to ask more clarifying questions would be better served by attending a Small-Group Mini-Lesson with the teacher.

How-To Sheets empower students to take responsibility for their own learning while offering them direct instruction through clear, step-by-step directions. At first, all students may follow a particular How-To Sheet to build a skill. Over time, students will select How-To Sheets based on the goals they've set. A student who has set a goal of reading three books by one author and then creating an author's page on a class website might, at the appropriate time, retrieve a How-To Sheet for creating a storyboard for an author's page and then, later, retrieve one for creating an author's page for a website. Over time, a teacher's collection of How-To Sheets offers students greater empowerment for their own learning.

Screencasts

Offering a printed sheet of directions allows students to follow visible steps and check them off. This level of responsibility builds executive function. However, with today's digitally oriented students, it is additionally powerful to create video-based How-To directions. This is relatively easy using screencasting software or capture software for interactive whiteboards.

As with a How-To Sheet, keep the video focused on a specific skill. Create your multimedia presentation with clear images and words that will trigger reminders for students. When recording, speak slowly. Whether or not you follow a script, you've already mastered the content, so you may be inclined to speak quickly. Cognitively, students need to take in information and make sense of it; so, speak slowly and deliberately. Anticipate questions students might ask and include them in the screencast.

Screencasts and similar videos allow students to receive direct instruction in skills and concepts. While they should not replace printed How-To Sheets, they are a great complement to the print version. If you have both printed and video learning activities, students will be able to choose, based on their learning style, and perhaps even use both. As with printed How-To Sheets, students can create screencasts for their peers for you to add to the classroom collection. If you teach primary students, you might ask teachers in upper grades, when they are teaching informational text and technical writing, to have their students design screencasts for the primary students.

Help Board

Shannon is working on calculating the area of a cylinder and is having difficulty. She cannot find a resource to help her; none of her peers are able to help her. She walks over to the Help Board and puts her name on it along with her challenge: area of a cylinder. She then moves on to other work for which she doesn't need help. Soon, when her teacher is finished with a conversation, he looks up to see Shannon's name and comes over to help her.

Your students could simply raise their hands and call out your name when they need help. Or they could:

◆ Identify that they cannot continue the current activity without help
◆ Check to see if there are any helpful resources in the Resource Area
◆ Look at the Expert Board to see if any Peer Experts have been identified for the skill
◆ Look at the Small-Group Mini-Lesson schedule to see if any skill-related lessons are scheduled for the day
◆ Ask some of their Home Group members or other peers
◆ Put their names on the Help Board for their teacher's assistance, and move on to another activity while waiting.

The bulleted list of alternates to raising one's hand or calling out for the teacher empowers students to take responsibility for their own learning and strengthens the executive function skill of *monitoring performance* in addition to many of the skills already introduced. It also helps teachers make their facilitation of learning deliberate and purposeful rather than reactionary and often interrupted.

Students need to learn the skill of being resourceful for success in college, career, and life. A Help Board causes students to pause, think through options, and generate ideas for how to get the help they need, before simply asking the teacher. You could use an erasable whiteboard or chart paper, or, in a 1:1 computing environment, you could create a digital Help Board.

Limited Resource Sign-Up

Whether it's a computer, electron microscope, or fish tank to observe, most classrooms have some resources that must be shared by students. The use of those resources could be designated and assigned by the teacher, or they could be allocated by a sign-up sheet for which students take responsibility. It may seem like a subtle difference, but having students take responsibility for signing up for a limited resource, rather than having the teacher assign it, builds executive function skills toward student empowerment.

Create a sign-up sheet to leave in the Resource Area. As students are deciding how to use their time to complete various instructional activities, they sign up for a time slot for any limited resources they may need. See Table 5.7 for an example of a sign-up sheet to use in an elementary, self-contained classroom; see Table 5.8 for an example for a departmentalized, class period sign-up.

You might want to provide students with a Small-Group Mini-Lesson on a particular skill. Given that the lesson is scheduled for a ten to fifteen-minute time slot, and there is a maximum number of students who may attend (I recommend no more than 6), this would be considered a limited resource. Students sign up for Small-Group Mini-Lessons in the Resource Area (see Table 5.9).

Table 5.7 Microscope Sign-Up: Elementary

Time	Name
9:00–9:20	
9:25–9:45	
9:50–10:10	
10:15–10:35	

Table 5.8 Microscope Sign-Up: Secondary

Time	Name
Mon 1:10–1:30	
Mon 1:33–1:53	
Tue 1:10–1:30	
Tue 1:35–1:55	

Table 5.9 Small-Group, Mini-Lesson Sign-Up Sheet

Title: _____

Time: _____

Participants

Overflow (I will schedule later in the day or another session)	

Learning Dashboard

Much like a car dashboard, a Learning Dashboard (paper or digital) presents information organized in a way that makes it easy to monitor one's progress. It offers a set of metrics one can use for reflection, goal-setting, improvement, and celebration. Have students create and maintain a dashboard using a digital document (see Table 5.10). Use of a dashboard helps build executive function skills related to empowerment.

You and your students can decide what important information should be on the dashboard for *monitoring progress* and *reflecting on goals*. In the case of the Learning Dashboard in Table 5.10, the students update the homework item daily to indicate if they brought in their completed homework. In this class, they take one or two quizzes a week, so they track the average of their quiz grades, which provides them with important formative assessment data from which to engage in *setting goals*. As they receive test and project grades, they calculate and record their average for the course. Each week, they identify three academic skills and three executive function skills on which they'll focus. As they begin working on a skill, they place a dash in the box; as they demonstrate some level of mastery, they place a check in the box, and as they demonstrate

Table 5.10 Lamar's Dashboard - English Per. 4

Week of 4/11	Daily Homework – missed Wednesday		Quiz Avg. – 89%		Course Avg. – 85%	
Skills Focus:	Poetry structure	✓	Figurative Lang.	★	Transitions	-
EF Focus:	Anticipating	★	Future Conseq.	✓	Reflecting	✓
Today's Work:	• Meet with Roger to discuss "The Highwayman"					
	• Attend Small-Group, Mini-Lessons on finding the shift in a poem					

full mastery they place a star in the box. Each week they *reflect on their goals* and *set new goals*. The final entry in this example is an identification of what they will be working on for the class period. They complete this the day before to be ready for the class period. This is one possible arrangement of data. You might want to include different criteria, such as attendance or behavior referrals, and even establish different criteria for different students. You might also want to have students include graphs of some of the data over time.

The Learning Dashboard helps students organize and focus on their goals and achievements. The related executive function skills are critical for succeeding at being empowered by the teacher to take responsibility for one's own learning.

Two-Pocket Folders

Eight-year-old Mason walks into his third-grade classroom, puts away his belongings, and sits down, waiting for the teacher's direction. The teacher then directs the class to generate adjectives to describe a porcupine, with a picture projected on a screen as a quick assessment, giving them 2 minutes to complete. She then has them turn to a partner to discuss their answers before discussing the answers with the class. She directs the students to get into groups to work on their group projects and calls five students to meet with her in a corner of the room where she will provide them with more detailed instruction. This is a common practice in many classrooms. Now juxtapose this with Sonia's experience:

Sonia walks into a classroom, puts away her belongings, retrieves a Two-Pocket Folder and begins to review its contents, particularly notes from the teacher regarding yesterday's work. She pulls out a "to do" list that she created and notes the first activity for her day, which is to watch a two-minute video on a topic that will help her in completing her group project. After watching it, she completes a reflection form, answering some questions about the content and its connection to her project. She then looks at an activity list the teacher has provided and makes some decisions about how she will use her time; she already knows that her team is planning to meet at 10:00. She writes down the activities she plans to complete before then; she notes that the teacher is offering a Small-Group Mini-Lesson on a skill that she will need so she goes to a sign-up board and adds her name, then she writes the time of that lesson on her activity list. Her next activity involves quiet reading, so she moves to a quiet corner of the room with soft seating and starts working.

These are two different classrooms offering students two different experiences. Both students will engage in meaningful academic work; both will work individually and in groups; both are completing academic projects with peers; both have access to instruction by the teacher. The difference lies in who has control over the minute-to-minute activities. In the first class-room, Mason only needs to attend to the teacher and compliantly follow her directions; in the second classroom—a *Learner-Active, Technology-Infused Classroom* (Sulla, 2011)—Sonia needs to draw on, and thus exercise and build, many executive function skills. For Sonia to manage her own learning experience, she must *set goals*, *manage time*, *self-assess*, *monitor her performance*, and *reflect on goals*.

While it may feel more comfortable for teachers to take overt control in the classroom, directing students throughout the day, teachers have the opportunity to build much-needed executive function skills by creating a set of structures that enable students, with the teacher's coaching and assis-tance, to successfully manage their own day. Sonia's teacher is using Student Folders, an Activity List of options, a Student Schedule that students must complete, a Small-Group Mini-Lesson sign-up board, and functional seating. These are structures in the classroom that will help students build executive function.

When teachers overtly direct students as to what to do when they enter the room through verbal or written directions, when they hand back papers to students, and when they manage work materials for their students, they inhibit students from practicing key executive function skills and, thus, from further building that part of the brain that controls executive function. Every action teachers take either supports teachers being in charge, thus enabling students to depend on them, or students being in charge, thus requiring students to strengthen executive function skills. While it may seem easier and faster to just manage the workflow for students, it is an important and worthwhile use of time to build structures that allow students to practice applying executive function skills to their daily lives.

Give each student a Two-Pocket Folder (or, in a 1:1 technology environ-ment, a digital folder) to organize activities and create a key communica-tion vehicle between student and teacher. Have students label one side (or one digital folder) "Work Completed" and the other "Work in Progress." Students leave the folders in the classroom so that the teacher can assess the completed work and comment on the work in progress. Students keep their current work and schedule in the folder for easy access. When students retrieve the folder, they first look at the "Work Completed" side and remove all work approved by the teacher. If the teacher requests additional work on any assignment, the student transfers that to the "Work in Progress" side.

When you introduce the Two-Pocket Folder, you will need to spend several days walking students through opening them up, checking the "Work Completed" side for notes from you, and so forth. The Two-Pocket Folder exercises all the executive function skills related to empowerment.

Summary for Embracing Empowerment (#EF_Empowerment)

Being empowered means being given the opportunity to make decisions, have a voice, and take responsibility for one's actions. Consider the executive function skills required and built by student development of empowerment. See how many activities and structures you can build into the day to enhance students' skills toward moving beyond dependence on you or others to taking charge of their own behaviors, thoughts, and actions.

Executive Function Skills:

- ◆ Catching and correcting errors
- ◆ Setting goals
- ◆ Managing time
- ◆ Self-assessing
- ◆ Monitoring performance
- ◆ Reflecting on goals

Activities:

- ◆ Recreating a Drawing
- ◆ Navigating a Maze
- ◆ How Much Time Did That Take?

Structures:

- ◆ Resource Area
- ◆ Anchor Charts

- ◆ Great Student Rubric
- ◆ How-To Sheets
- ◆ Screencasts
- ◆ Help Board
- ◆ Limited Resource Signup
- ◆ Learning Dashboard
- ◆ Two-Pocket Folder

References

Duckworth, A. (2016). *Grit: The power of passion and perseverance*. New York: Scribner.

Dweck, C. S. (2006). *Mindset: The new psychology of success*. New York: Random House.

Sulla, N. (2011). *Students taking charge: Inside the Learner-Active, Technology-Infused Classroom*. New York: Routledge.

Sulla, N. (2015). *It's not what you teach but how: 7 insights to making the CCSS work for you*. New York: Routledge.

6

Developing Efficacy
(#EF_Efficacy)

Learning eventually outfits one to carry out a plan of action, achieve goals, and make a difference. While empowerment is bestowed upon you by someone else, efficacy comes from within: it is your own ability to decide upon a desired outcome and make it happen. It is at the core of successful, effective living.

Efficacy requires an even more sophisticated executive function skillset than the overarching life skills presented in the preceding chapters, including (see also Table 6.1):

- ◆ Working towards a goal (Planning)
- ◆ Organizing actions and thoughts (Planning)
- ◆ Considering future consequences in light of current action (Planning)
- ◆ Making hypotheses, deductions, and inferences (Reasoning)
- ◆ Applying former approaches to new situations (Reasoning)
- ◆ Defining a problem (Problem Solving)
- ◆ Analyzing (Problem Solving)
- ◆ Creating mental images (Problem Solving)
- ◆ Generating possible solutions (Problem Solving)
- ◆ Anticipating (Problem Solving)
- ◆ Predicting outcomes (Problem Solving)
- ◆ Evaluating (Problem Solving).

In the classroom, you can help students achieve a sense of efficacy by establishing a classroom culture of efficacy that embraces *creativity* and *problem-solving*.

Table 6.1 Executive Function Skills Related to Efficacy

Planning	Setting goals	*Problem*	Defining a problem
	Managing time	*Solving*	Analyzing
	Working towards a goal		Creating mental images
	Organizing actions and thoughts		Generating possible solutions
	Considering future consequences		Anticipating
	in light of current action		Predicting outcomes
			Evaluating
Reasoning	Making hypotheses, deductions,		
	and inferences		
	Applying former approaches to		
	new situations		

More than a set of activities for building executive function skills, a culture is a set of shared beliefs, values, assumptions, symbols, and traditions that support growth in every aspect of a student's life. To break down that definition down into an example of a culture of *creativity* and *problem-solving*:

◆ Belief—All students can learn to take charge of lives and make a difference for others
◆ Value—Students should engage in unstructured time across the week that encourages them to dream, invent, play, and foster their creative side
◆ Assumptions—If students are given the freedom and support, they can devise a plan to accomplish a feasible goal and carry it out
◆ Symbols—"Ideate" boards where students post interesting ideas for solving real-world problems
◆ Traditions—At the end of their year, students write letters to the incoming students sharing their tips for being efficacious, creative problem-solvers.

Creating a culture requires you to challenge your beliefs, values, and assumptions; it requires you to build symbols and traditions. The first two sections of the chapter will address creating a culture of *creativity* and of *problem-solving* toward building the executive function skills in students that will support efficacy. The third section will offer you structures to utilize to support your efforts.

Creating a Culture of Creativity

Creativity is the generation of new ideas and processes, imagining what does not yet exist in your worldview. It is a mental process of connecting things in new ways, of synthesizing. While many use the term as a personality characteristic, even going as far to propose that it is innate; in fact, *creativity* is an executive function skill. *Creativity* can be developed.

Apple Computer founder Steve Jobs (1996) shared in an interview that: "Creativity is just connecting things. When you ask creative people how they did something, they feel a little guilty because they didn't really do it, they just saw something. It seemed obvious to them after a while. That's because they were able to connect experiences they've had and synthesize new things." To describe *creativity* in terms of its prerequisite executive function skills, including some previously discussed, *creativity* depends on one's ability to consider current experiences, concepts, and ideas, and *analyze, think about multiple concepts simultaneously, shift focus from one event to another, see multiple sides to a situation, change perspective,* and *create mental images.* Through those skills, one can make connections more easily.

In describing the process of *creativity*, Koestler (1964) coined the term "bisociation" as the process of taking two ideas that seemingly do not connect, and connecting them to create something new. The electric light is an example of bisociation. The harnessing of electric power occurred in the mid-1700s and led to many inventions, including the electric locomotive, telephone, and telegraph. While light was certainly a known concept at the time, it was relegated to stoves and candles and had not been connected to the concept of electricity. It was Humphry Davy who, in 1809, after having invented a battery, accidentally discovered that when connecting wires to the battery and a piece of carbon, the carbon glowed; he made the connection that he might be able to produce light from electricity. Suddenly, two seemingly disconnected concepts were now connected. This caused the generation of many ideas and prototypes for a light bulb, which Edison finally succeeded in perfecting in 1878.

In order to "connect the dots" and make connections, one must have a lot of experiences to draw upon. The more one has experienced, the more likely one will be able to make connections between and among ideas. Sadly, extensive, early experiences can be lacking in some students' lives, leaving them at a disadvantage against their more experienced peers. The toddler who is surrounded by a variety of play objects, interacts often with people, and is taken to various places is building a wealth of experiences from which to draw to make connections. Financially, not all parents can fill their children's lives with such vast experiences. Classrooms, therefore, should offer students a wealth of experiences, including varied furniture, manipulatives, texts, videos, images, tools, sounds, experiments, field trips, and so forth, to build equity in this area. For students who are geographically limited, not inclined to visit other parts of the country or world, videos can offer a glimpse of life in other places, building the students' frame of reference.

A first step, then, toward building a culture of *creativity* is to simply fill students' day with varied experiences. Consider experiences related to your content that draw on the five senses of sight, sound, touch, taste, and smell. Fill the room and the day with them. If you're teaching adjectives, have a variety of objects available to describe through the senses, such as a bell, drum, castanets, sandpaper, cotton, wax paper, lemon, chicory, salt, sugar, potpourri, coffee beans, cinnamon sticks, hyacinth, and so forth, letting students experience descriptive words through their senses. If you're teaching about a particular time in history, have music of the historical time being studied playing in the background as students enter the classroom, include timelines and images on the walls, and/or secure artifacts from a lending museum. Present your content through as many of the senses as you can.

Keep in mind, however, that it is difficult to be creative when asked to complete assignments that have one right answer and follow a prescribed format. Creating a culture of *creativity* requires creating opportunities for students to be creative. Reflect on the types of assignments and activities you offer students. Ensure that some of them allow for *creativity*. On national crayon day, an elementary teacher asked students to generate and write about an idea for a new Crayola crayon color. A French teacher asked students to use Google Earth to find an apartment location in France and write about what it would be like to live there. A math teacher asked students to create increasingly complex, and therefore difficult, word problems for a game, focusing on the use of percent of increase/decrease. As you engage students in open-ended problem-solving and application of content, you provide myriad opportunities for students to exercise their *creativity*.

Behaviors Shared by Creative People

In their book, *Wired to Create: Unraveling the Mysteries of the Creative Mind* (2015), authors Scott Barry Kaufman and Carolyn Gregoire share eighteen behaviors typical of highly creative people. Teachers can foster the development of these behaviors in the classroom, building a culture of *creativity*. Following are nine of the identified behaviors of highly creative people that you can easily foster in the classroom:

Highly Creative People Daydream

Letting your mind wander isn't always a bad thing; in fact, daydreaming stimulates the same part of the brain that is associated with imagination. For elementary students, build "daydream" time into the schedule! Encourage students to just sit alone somewhere, eyes open or closed, and just let their minds drift beyond the classroom. They can later write about their day-dreams in a journal. For middle- and high-school students, encourage them to daydream either in school or at home, to just let their minds drift beyond their schoolwork. They can keep a journal or engage in a group blog on "The Mind's Wanderings."

Obviously, you don't want students daydreaming during your lessons, but if you build the day and week as a combination of time spent engaged in lessons with you and time spent engaging in independent, pairs, and group learning activities, students will still be able to schedule time to let their minds wander. The time they spend daydreaming may actually enhance their academic achievement, as it is in daydreaming that one draws on experiences and makes connections.

Design your physical space to allow for a variety of functional areas, including group spaces and individual spaces: spaces for work, discussion, and thinking. Study carrels, Adirondack chairs, and soft seating areas can allow students to spend some alone time in their work or thoughts. A primary teacher built a loft in her room allowing students to sit underneath or climb up top for quiet time.

Highly Creative People Observe Everything

The world is full of possibilities, and creative people tap into that by observing everything around them. Teach students to observe. For elementary students, set up learning centers with items for them to observe, such as a terrarium, fish tank, classroom pets, photographs, paintings, objects, and more. Have them note everything they see and hear during a specified period. Have them observe experiments and note everything they see, hear, smell, taste, and touch. For homework, have them observe something outside. For secondary students, encourage them to keep an observation journal (paper or digital) to record observable moments they encounter outside of school. Offer a homework assignment of just stopping and recording what they see on the street, in a park, by the ocean, on a mountain, in a store, etc. There's a great weekend or vacation assignment: observe.

Highly Creative People Work the Hours That Work for Them

While you might not be able to fully implement this concept, given that schools tend to have set hours that students attend, you can give students choice over when they accomplish various tasks in the classroom. If a student wants to read now and conduct an experiment later, so be it! Giving students autonomy with their time will allow students to create a workflow that works for them. For more on designing classrooms where students enjoy greater autonomy, see *Students Taking Charge* (Sulla, 2011). For secondary students, virtual courses can allow more flexibility for them to engage at times that work for them.

Highly Creative People Fail Up

Got Grit? (Duckworth, 2016) Help students learn from failure and persist to achieve success. Share stories of inspirational people who learned from their failures, such as inventor Thomas Edison who is reported to have said, in response to his failures in attempting to make a battery, that he didn't fail; he just knows 10,000 ways not to make a battery. Oprah Winfrey was fired from her job as a television co-anchor but went on to become a successful business woman with news and television shows, a magazine, and a television network. Walt Disney was fired from his job at a newspaper, apparently for lacking imagination; his first animation business ended in bankruptcy; and MGM rejected his idea of Mickey Mouse, claiming a giant mouse on the screen would frighten women. Michael Jordan, now considered one of the greatest basketball players of all time, was cut from his high school basketball team. Steven Spielberg was twice rejected from the University of Southern California, his first choice for film school. He went on to be a highly prolific and successful filmmaker and USC awarded him an honorary degree in 1994. Congressional representative Barbara Jordan lost her bid for election as president of her freshman class in college; she then lost her bid for student body president. Her freshman debate coach told her she wasn't good at speaking extemporaneously. She went on to become the first African-American elected to the Texas Senate and the first African-American woman from a southern state elected to Congress, known for her powerful speeches; she was eventually honored with the Presidential Medal of Freedom.

Encourage students to take risks in their work and learn from their mistakes, rather than taking the "safe" route. Lead students to question why a particular approach did not work and determine what they can learn from the failure. Keep a "Failing Forward" bulletin board or class journal where students can share their challenges and breakthroughs. The pursuit of grit should be part of the classroom culture, with teachers being transparent about sharing ideas that did not work from personal experience.

Highly Creative People Ask the Big Questions

Why? How? These are the questions of creative thinkers, the continually curious. Model asking the big questions when addressing curricular topics. Encourage students to consider content and ask questions about why and how things work or are the way they are. While at times, students' questions can veer off the curricular path, take care to foster curiosity. A Parking Lot can be a place for students to post those questions that may not relate to the curriculum matter at hand, but can be documented for later retrieval. Include time for students to discuss those ideas as a class, in small groups, or in pairs. Create a "Big Questions" bulletin board or journal for students to share answers to big questions they pursue.

Highly Creative People View Life as an Opportunity for Self Expression

Encourage students to share their interests, desires, and personal qualities through their work. Use wall space and bulletin boards to allow students to create personal interpretations of curricular content with their own unique spin. Avoid using templates that have all students generating work that looks like everyone else's. You can still have the "non-negotiables" in, say, a lab report, but why not let students develop their own unique approach to reporting on that experiment? As students work to provide solutions to open-ended curricular problems, allow flexibility for them to share their ideas in a variety of ways, such as an essay, skit, infographic, video, website, news article, and so forth. After all, unless you're trying to teach a particular presentation style, what you care about is demonstration of content. Encourage *creativity* in that.

Highly Creative People Get Out of Their Own Heads

Like daydreaming, creative minds often intentionally take another person's perspective to see a situation from outside themselves. Where possible, encourage students to record their own viewpoints and then consider another's viewpoint. A popular activity in teaching the U.S. Civil War is to have students write a newspaper article from the perspective of a northern soldier, southern soldier, enslaved person, plantation owner, northern factory worker, and so forth. When teaching about community helpers, have students take on the perspective of a postal worker, police officer, or firefighter in a role play.

Highly Creative People Connect the Dots

Highly creative people generate possibilities, making connections among the known to create the unknown. This requires a combination of ample experiences and the ability to make those connections. While this skill relies on several executive function skills introduced earlier, such as *identifying same and different, categorizing information, thinking about multiple concepts simultaneously*; it also requires the skill of *applying former approaches to new situations*, a key executive function skill for efficacy.

Provide students with opportunities to consider how multiple items connect. Give them a collection of items (or ask them to take out items they have on hand) and have them write a story about them or use them to develop a prototype for a new product. Have them read multiple articles on a topic and decide how the concepts and information connect. Let them play and invent. Make time for dot-connecting!

Highly Creative People Make Time for Mindfulness

Mindfulness meditation is becoming popular in schools everywhere. It can start as simply as sitting comfortably, closing your eyes, and paying attention to nothing other than your own breath. With hands on stomach, feel and hear yourself breathing in and out. Work to let your mind be empty of thoughts. Whenever a thought pops into your head, don't dwell on it or become frustrated; just let it go. Be mindful of your breathing. MRI scans show that after eight weeks of regular mindfulness meditation, the part of the brain that handles the "fight or flight" response begins to shrink, and the prefrontal cortex increases in density (Holze et al., 2011). This is an important shift in the brain for efficacy. Spend time teaching your students mindfulness.

Habit as the Enemy of Creativity

Part of preparing students for their future is to help them take responsibility for their learning, developing strong habits for academic success. Habits are controlled, in part, by the prefrontal cortex: the command center for executive function. They are critical for academic success. While schools tend to focus on building habits in students, it is important to frame the value of habits as being necessary but not sufficient for an efficacious life. The sparring partner of habits is *creativity*. Habits are learned and repetitive. They are restraining and rigid by necessity. *Creativity* is more subconscious, novel, unrestrained, and flexible. While habits will help tremendously in supporting productivity and effectiveness, they will squelch *creativity*. Therefore, it is important to provide times for creative thinking absent of constraining habits.

In other words, the list of executive function skills does not always work well together. Children often come to school leading with *creativity* and curiosity; schools work hard to build their skills for planning, inhibitory control, self-awareness, and reasoning. The executive function skills that fall under those categories may inhibit *creativity*.

When working to build *creativity*, it is important to stimulate the brain toward those categories that support *creativity*, and avoid stimulating the other areas. For example, when students are brainstorming ideas, refrain from asking them to self-assess or organize those ideas. Fostering *creativity* means temporarily letting go of the constraints of organization and perfectionism. Build a classroom culture in which students realize there is a time for *creativity*, which requires divergent thinking, and a time for reasoning, planning, and perfection, skills that require more convergent thinking.

Genius Hour

You may have heard about how Google encourages its engineers to allocate 20 percent of their time to pursue project ideas about which they are passionate. This time has led to some of Google's successful products and offerings. Schools have been increasingly implementing this approach with the addition of Genius Hour to the school schedule. You can learn more at www.geniushour.com. The key is to provide students with time to pursue their passions by exploring ideas that are of interest to them. While you may be inclined to structure the time, be mindful of how you do. Guiding questions will work. Asking students to keep a journal is fine. But the ideas really should emanate from students, and then they should be allowed to explore and report in on what they've accomplished. Depending on your classroom design, you can designate a Genius Hour built into the week or month, or you can allow students to build it into their schedule when it works for them.

Creating a Culture of Problem-Solving

There are two types of problems that students are asked to solve in schools. Most prevalent are closed-ended problems that have one right answer. Students must recall skills and concepts learned and apply them to arrive at the correct solution. Once you know how to add, you can calculate how many more apples Josh has than Aisha, given there are a total of ten apples and Aisha has three. Once you understand the structure of an atom and how to read the periodic table, you can draw molecular models of compounds. Once you understand how to recognize a main idea from supporting details, you can read texts and better understand the message.

While closed-ended problems have a place in school, open-ended problems require significantly more executive function. Design a habitat to house a pair of giraffes at the school; propose a design for a playground that will be appropriate for students from pre-K through fifth grade; write a new ending to the book you just read; propose a solution to greatly reduce the amount of plastic currently in our oceans; write an original song to inspire people regarding a global problem of interest to you; propose a solution to quell civil wars; or identify an alternative fuel source. These are all open-ended problems. While there are criteria that must be addressed, there is not just one, right solution. In solving open-ended problems, students draw upon existing knowledge but must propose a solution to a problem that may have many plausible solutions. While solutions-finding requires skills that are also applied to closed-ended problems, open-ended problem solvers must broaden their minds to myriad possibilities to solve the problem.

Problem solving is a category of executive function that includes the skills of *defining a problem, analyzing, creating mental images, generating possible solutions, anticipating, predicting outcomes,* and *evaluating.* For more complex, open-ended problems, a step-by-step design process with guiding questions can offer students a framework for solutions finding.

You may have heard the term design process discussed as a key tool for the engineering aspect of a STEM program. The reality is that any authentic, open-ended problem, in any subject area, lends itself to a design process. By way of background, the scientific method, which is regularly taught in schools, seeks to explain that which exists. Students consider a situation, make a hypothesis, and then conduct experiments to prove or disprove their hypothesis. In the process, they discover realities about the scientific world. The design process seeks to create that which does not exist.

Suppose I notice that my plant that is placed farthest from natural light is looking frail, whereas the same type of plant in the window with the most sunlight is thriving. I may hypothesize that this type of plant needs direct sunlight. To test my hypothesis, I would plant several and place them in three locations: the window with direct sunlight, a desk with indirect sunlight, and in the dark closet. Keeping all other conditions, such as watering, the same; I find that the plant without light dies, the one in direct sunlight thrives the most. I've just proven a scientific truth about this species of plant: it thrives best in direct sunlight. That's the scientific method; and while it is most often applied to science, it could be applied to a variety of other subjects as well.

Alternatively, suppose I wake up one morning and my back is in pain; I can't bend over without significant pain; but I have to put on my socks! I head to the kitchen to see what I can find and I grab some long barbecue tongs. Sure enough, I manage to put on my socks without bending over. That is design process; I've invented a solution to address my problem.

Whereas much of schooling is about mastering the "known" and proving that which is known to be true in the world, a design process is about inventing the "unknown" and creating that which does not yet exist, as in, a solution to a yet unsolved problem. The balancing of habit and *creativity,* of the known and unknown, of the existing and new is a personal quality that leads to a sense of efficacy.

Design Process

IDE Corp.'s design process is depicted as an informational graphic in Figure 6.1 (see Appendices I, J, and K for a set of possible graphic organizers to use with students.)

If implemented deliberately and purposefully, the design process can build significant executive function.

Figure 6.1 (c) 2016, IDE corp.

The design process involves both divergent and convergent thinking. In divergent thinking, you generate possibilities, think non-linearly, and open yourself to new pathways of thinking. In convergent thinking, you narrow your focus, think more linearly, and seek the right answer. The combination of both is what makes the design process successful.

In IDE Corp.'s design process videos (located in the YouTube channel: www.youtube.com/user/LATIClassroom), we use the example of a man who invented edible cutlery in India. It all begins with the "mic-drop" statement, "Each year, 120 billion pieces of disposable plastic cutlery are discarded in India." That is a compelling reason to tackle this problem!

The first step in the design process is to Formulate the problem, which includes empathy: seeing the situation from the perspective of those most affected. What is the current reality? In the case of the plastic cutlery problem, it's the fact that 120 billion pieces are disposed of annually. Who is affected by the problem and how? What is the ideal situation? What will happen if the problem is not solved? These are the questions students answer during the formulate step. Pursuing the answers builds the executive function skills of *defining a problem, creating mental images, predicting outcomes, considering future consequences in light of current action*; and *making hypotheses, deductions, and inferences*. The Formulate step has students defining the problem situation by researching it and mapping out, if applicable, the consequences of non-action that have occurred over several years and may occur in the future. If students were solving India's plastic cutlery challenge, they would move between divergent (generating questions) and convergent (finding answers) thinking processes to understand the realities of the situation. To guide students, place formulation questions on a single card or graphic organizer or write out the set of questions on a Direction Sheet.

Once students have a clear understanding of the problem, the next step is to Explore it. Students engage with subject area content to build knowledge; it's a study of the "known." This is where much of your course content will be presented and will, thus, most likely take up a significant amount of time during the unit of study. The Explore step requires a combination of divergent thinking, in which students generate questions, and convergent thinking, in which they find known answers. You may wish to have students keep a design notebook. You might also develop a graphic organizer to help with previously discussed executive function skills, such as *categorization* of content and *organizing thoughts and actions*, depending on the executive function needs of the student. For young students exploring an animal, for example, you might create a graphic organizer that includes the categories: Description, Habitat, Food, and Life Cycle. For an older student, you might include categories such as Statistics, Facts, Anecdotes, Hypotheses, etc.

The Explore step requires students to employ the previously discussed executive function skills of *shifting from one event to another* by *focusing* on the research medium and then taking steps to write down the information. Additionally, students will further strengthen the ability to *store and manipulate visual and verbal information* as they work through the research, noting information already captured versus new information. You can guide students during this step with graphic organizers and How-To Sheets for conducting information searches, inquiry based research, and experiments.

Once the student has sufficient understanding of the content related to the problem, the next step in the design process is to Ideate: generate lots of possible solutions. This step focuses exclusively on divergent thinking and builds the executive function skills of *creativity*, *generating possible solutions*, *creating mental images*, and *applying former approaches to new situations*. The key is to generate ideas without judging them; no idea is a bad idea at this point. Students optimally work together to generate ideas, each bringing his/her own content area mastery to the process. To spark *creativity*, offer students prompts to make connections, such as, "What other ideas or products seem similar?" or "Does this resemble any other problem you've solved?"

Next, the students move on to Sift through the ideas to identify the best. This step focuses primarily on the convergent thinking process and calls for graphic organizers to analyze the information, thus building executive function. It might include categories such as: Could This Really Happen? Would It Solve the Problem? Would It Create Other Problems? How Would It Affect Everyone or Everything Involved? For older students, the categories might be: Feasibility, Positive Impact, Negative Impact, and Unintended Consequences. In the case of the cutlery problem, the solutions-finder decided he could bake edible cutlery that could be consumed or, if thrown away, would biodegrade in four days. If approached purposefully, the Sift step activates the executive function skills of *analysis*; *predicting outcomes*; *anticipating, evaluating*; *creating mental images*; *considering future consequences in light of current action; generating possible solutions; working towards a goal; organizing thoughts and actions; making hypotheses, deductions, and inferences;* and *applying former approaches to new situations.*

The next step, Simulate, involves testing the idea. That includes creating a prototype, mock-up, storyboard, or other product that can be tested. In the case of a habitat or playground design, it might be a drawing or model. In the case of a new ending to the book, it would be the actual writing. In the case of an alternative fuel source, it might be an infographic or descriptive paper. In the case of a song it would be writing the actual song to share with others for feedback. In the case of a solution for microplastics in the ocean, it might be a simulated removal of microplastics from salt water combined with an action plan. In the case of the plastic cutlery, it was the baking of edible cutlery. Clearly, if a student is attempting to move a load of particular poundage up a flight of stairs, the prototype can undergo testing through the Simulate step. In the case of other products mentioned above, the student may have to seek the advice of experts to determine the strength of the solution or survey an audience to determine how they felt about an idea or performance. This step involves some divergent thinking of the best way to simulate the solution but focuses mostly on convergent thinking to create a test case for the solution.

Finally, once the student has a working solution, the next step is to Advocate for it; that is, select the appropriate audience and present the solution. Students decide how to make the case for their solution and how to present it. It might be a paper or editorial, a website or multimedia presentation, a speech, a performance, a video, and so forth. The most powerful situations are those in which the audience is other than the teacher and students in the classroom. This step, like the Simulate step, requires some divergent thinking but is mostly convergent in nature, resulting in a solid presentation of the solution to an audience, which could be in person, through video or print, and so forth. Second- grade students studying citizenship designed a plan to attract visitors to their downtown area, creating brochures they delivered to the local Main Street organization. Middle school students designed plans for a biking and walking path for a new bridge being constructed and presented them to the bridge committee. High school environmental science students developed a plan for their new high school that would have the least human impact on climate change and pitched them to the district's strategic planning committee. The key is for students to advocate for their ideas to an authentic audience: a person or organization.

Throughout the process students might find the need to return to a prior step; the process is a system of interdependent processes, as depicted in Figure 6.2.

Figure 6.2

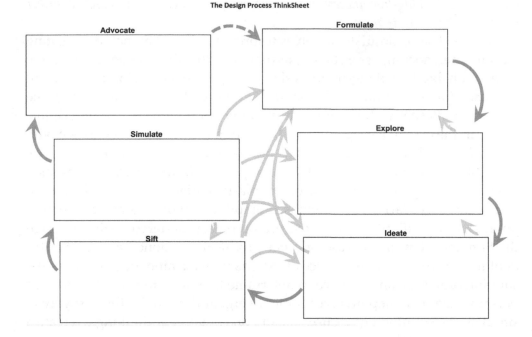

The Design Process ThinkSheet

Solving open-ended problems is an activity in which students can engage across the disciplines and, thus, should be included to some degree in all subject area studies. The design process offers a methodology to problem solving that exercises, and thus strengthens, a large number of executive function skills. Effective *problem-solving* skills are key to attaining efficacy.

Structures

Creating a culture of *creativity* and *problem solving* will position your students to believe they can make a difference in their life and the lives of others. It will build the executive function skills needed to be a problem-finder, innovator, and entrepreneur (Sulla, 2015). However, it requires students to identify a goal or project, develop a plan for success, and carry out that plan, adjusting along the way based on feedback and reflection. These skills are best fostered through classroom structures. A fourth-grade teacher labelled the entry wall to her classroom with the title, "Ways We Are Changing the World." She then mapped out a timeline from September through June and students posted the problems they were solving across the year. The culture of *creativity* and *problem-solving* is evident as soon as you walk in the room. Consider how you can make that culture transparent in your room. Following are some that structures that all teachers can incorporate into the classroom.

External Brain

One challenge for students as they build executive function is maintaining focus and organization over the long-term. When students are working on a longer-term report or project, an "external brain" can help students build an understanding of the need to maintain and organize information throughout the project. Have students keep track of information they find, with citations, on index cards, then placing them in a shoe box or large, manila envelope. Students can create a digital version as well. The External Brain allows students to keep track of information that they may not readily remember over the course of the unit of study. When it's time to write the report or work on the project, students "dump their brains" on the table and get to work organizing the information. It's a non-threatening way to help students maintain and organize information when they might otherwise feel frustrated and inadequate. Once the information is retrieved, they have to *work towards a goal, organize actions and thoughts*, and *evaluate* the information they've collected.

Learning Contracts

A learning contract is an agreement between a student and teacher in which the student commits to achieving certain goals related to academics, work habits, and behaviors. This structure serves as a tangible work schedule and the starting point for students developing and implementing a plan, foundational for achieving a sense of efficacy.

For young students, write up a contract for a single day or a contract for recurring actions over the course of the week. For older students, write up a contract for a week or the length of a unit or project.

In addition to typical contract information such as the student's name, date of contract, date for fulfillment of contract, and places for the teacher and student, and optionally the parent, to sign, you'll want at least a section that details the goals for the student. You may have more sections, such as:

- ◆ Teacher-established goals: The teacher sets one to three goals for the student related to academics (e.g., write one book review this week), work habits (e.g., bring paper and pen to all small-group lessons), or behaviors (work without distracting or interrupting others from their work).
- ◆ Student-established goals: The student sets one to three goals related to academics, work habits, or behaviors.
- ◆ Teacher responsibilities: The teacher determines with the student what the teacher should do to support the student in the fulfilment

of the contract. This may be as general as, "provide learning opportunities" for related goals, or as specific as, "check off my goal sheet each time I arrive at a small-group lesson prepared with paper and pen."

◆ Contract fulfillment: This describes what the student will receive upon successful completion of the contract, which could be a grade or some sort of privilege. Note: I never recommend skipping homework as a reward, as that sends a negative message about the purpose and power of homework.

◆ Contract violation: This describes what the student will do if the contract is not successfully completed.

For students who are weak in executive function and/or work habits, the contract can provide a very concrete focal point for student action and reflection. In creating and fulfilling the contract, the student will exercise the executive function skills of *working towards a goal, considering future consequences in light of current action*, and *self-assessing*. Additionally, working with contracts supports the previously discussed executive function skills of *monitoring performance, reflecting on goals, attending to a person or activity, initiating a task*, and *persisting in a task*. For older students, a contract can serve as a precursor to career situations in which they must complete a project to certain requirements, also requiring executive function skills to create and fulfill.

Create a form that students complete and you review and sign, to make it easier to manage the process. You might decide to only offer contracts at designated times or make them available to students who are interested or need to build related skills.

Grit Area

Efficacy, the belief that you can develop a plan to achieve a goal and meet with success, requires one to have grit. Angela Duckworth (2016) defines grit as a "combination of passion and perseverance" (p. 8). It is an attitude of never giving up, of persisting through the challenges to achieve greatness. Gritty people set challenges for themselves that stretch beyond what they've already achieved, and then they make it happen. Efficacy and grit go hand in hand.

More and more schools are focusing on this concept of grit and helping students develop a gritty attitude. While there are many strategies teachers can employ along these lines, a related structure is a Grit Area. Clearly, you don't *need* a physical location to build grit, but it can help to offer students a concrete look at some of the components of grit. Have you ever seen a

Table 6.2 Grit Tracking: My stretch goal/activity is:

Date	Progress	Challenges and How I Overcame Them

student give up on a puzzle, game, physical challenge, or other challenge? They may feel like they're going to fail, so why try? They may lack the executive function skill of *persisting in a task*.

Create an area in or adjacent to your room that is filled with academic challenges and puzzles that would be a stretch for your students. Have students schedule some time in the Grit Room daily or weekly to focus on enhancing their grittiness. Students can identify a stretch goal or activity within the Grit Area or decide on one themselves. Their job is to focus solely on that goal for a period of time that they are in the Grit Area and record their experiences. How are they progressing? What breakthroughs have they made? What challenges are they facing that make them want to give up? How do they push through? Table 6.2 is an example of a tracking card you can use with students to focus them on the importance of grit in pursuing their goals.

Clearly, grit refers to a characteristic you demonstrate throughout your day, and life; however, the Grit Area is a fun way to focus on the importance of learning to persevere. Many of the skills needed for achieving stretch goals fall under the executive function umbrella, so students' prefrontal cortexes will be getting a workout. Depending on the size and location of your Grit Area, you can include some common activities that help energize the prefrontal cortex, such as:

◆ Deep Breaths—Hang a poster that directs the student to take five deep breaths before continuing.
◆ Exercise—Hang a poster that directs the student to complete ten jumping jacks for some quick oxygen flow to the brain.
◆ Water—Direct students to drink water to keep hydrated. The brain is very sensitive to dehydration, even mild dehydration that is the result of going four to eight hours without water. Working memory is adversely affected as water levels decrease.

If you establish a Grit Area to draw attention to this important concept for efficacy, you can draw on students' experiences during conversations. Ask students what obstacles they experienced while working on their stretch goal or activity and how they overcame them. You can use these experiences to spur students on to apply those same strategies throughout the day whenever they are faced with an obstacle and want to give up. While you don't need a grit area to build grit, a physical area, particularly in the elementary grades and with older students who suffer from executive dysfunction, focuses students on taking deliberate steps to being gritty.

Summary for Developing Efficacy (#EF_Efficacy)

Efficacy refers to one's ability to set a goal, make a plan, and carry it out to a successful outcome. Rather than being led by others to achieve, it's the ability to lead one's self. Executive function skills play an important role in becoming efficacious.

Executive Function Skills:

◆ Working towards a goal
◆ Organizing actions and thoughts
◆ Considering future consequences in light of current action
◆ Making hypotheses, deductions, and inferences
◆ Applying former approaches to new situations
◆ Defining a problem
◆ Analyzing
◆ Creating mental images
◆ Generating possible solutions
◆ Anticipating
◆ Predicting outcomes
◆ Evaluating

Create a Culture of Creativity:

◆ Build time, space, and opportunities for students to engage in the habits shared by highly creative people.
  ◆ Creative People Daydream
  ◆ Creative People Observe Everything
  ◆ Creative People Work the Hours That Work for Them

- ◆ Creative People Fail Up
- ◆ Creative People Ask the Big Questions
- ◆ Creative People View Life as an Opportunity for Self Expression
- ◆ Creative People Get Out of Their Own Heads
- ◆ Creative People Connect the Dots
- ◆ Creative People Make Time for Mindfulness.
- ◆ While building habits is an important part of executive function and personal success, habits may be the enemy of creativity that keep one constrained. Be sure to promote creativity activities that free students from habits.

Create a Culture of Problem-Solving:

- ◆ Consider authentic, open-ended problems to pose to your students to engage them in content-related problem-solving at the start of a unit of study.
- ◆ Use a Design Process:
  - ◆ Formulate
  - ◆ Explore
  - ◆ Ideate
  - ◆ Sift
  - ◆ Simulate
  - ◆ Advocate

Structures:

- ◆ External Brain
- ◆ Learning Contracts
- ◆ Grit Area.

References

Duckworth, A. (2016). *Grit: The power of passion and perseverance*. New York: Scribner.

Holze, B. K., Carmody, J., Vangel, M., Congleton, C., Yerramsetti, S. M., Gard, T., Lazar, S. (2011, January). Mindfulness practice leads to increases in regional brain gray matter density. *Psychiatry research: Neuroimaging*, 191(1), 36–43. doi: http://dx.doi.org/10.1016/j.pscychresns.2010.08.006

Jobs, S. (1996). "Steve Jobs: The next insanely great thing." Interview by Gary Wolf in Wired. February 1, 1996.

Kaufman, S. B., Gregoire, C. (2015). *Wired to create: Unraveling the mysteries of the creative mind*. New York: Penguin.

Koestler, A. (1964). *The act of creation*. London: Hutchinson.

Sulla, N. (2011). *Students taking charge: Inside the Learner-Active, Technology-Infused Classroom*. New York: Routledge.

Sulla, N. (2015). *It's not what you teach but how: 7 insights to making the CCSS work for you*. New York: Routledge.

Demonstrating Leadership
(#EF_Leadership)

If you have a personal sense of efficacy such that you can tackle challenges and see a plan through to completion, you can achieve far greater results if you can lead others to join you or build their own sense of efficacy. Think of some leaders you've known, whether those you personally followed or those written about throughout history. What was it about them that endowed them with such a presence that caused others to follow?

The term "leadership" has many definitions, but generally those definitions have the following characteristics in common: the ability to inspire and influence people. Inspiration enables you to ignite a passion in others for causes and journeys, to keep people moving beyond the obstacles, to help others focus and believe in something bigger than themselves. Influence enables you to gain the respect and support of others toward a greater, common goal. It allows others to follow you with belief and trust. As depicted in a quote by Joel Arthur Barker (1992), "A Leader is a person you will follow to a place you wouldn't go by yourself" (p. 163).

Some use their leadership skills in small ways, such as leading their own children or friends in making good decisions for their personal welfare. Some use them in large ways, leading organizations, companies, and countries. Regardless of the leader's breadth of influence, all the executive function skills are critical in supporting the development of leadership skills; however, they combine into what I will call the super-skills of empathy, confidence, vision, courage, integrity, intuition, and systems-thinking (Figure 7.1). As you focus

Figure 7.1 (c) 2016, IDE corp.

on building your students' executive function skills, consider how you can provide opportunities for students to exercise these super-skills for leadership, keeping focus on the contributing executive function skills that shape them.

You may think that with high-stakes testing and the need to focus on building academic skills, you don't have time to address the super-skills of leadership. Consider that these super-skills also support academic achievement, when achievement is defined as understanding and application and not mere procedural memorization. Students need confidence and courage in attempting more difficult academic challenges; vision will help them persist in their academic pursuits; empathy, intuition, and systems thinking are key skills for problem-solving; and integrity will steer them toward putting in the time and energy to mastering content. Focus on building students' leadership super-skills, which will in turn strengthen executive function.

Empathy

Empathy is the ability to put oneself in the place of another person to understand what that person is experiencing and feeling. Unlike sympathy, there is not a power differential in empathy. You are, in your mind, one with the other person or living being, able to better perceive the effect a situation is having on others. As an example, if you empathize with people in a part of the world that lacks ready access to water, you can imagine what it must feel like to have to guard every drop, walk long distances to a well to retrieve the water, and be continuously mindful of the lessening supply to plan for the next trip. You do not feel sorry for the people; you understand the situation and see it from their perspective. Empathy is much more powerful than sympathy; it is the spark that ignites great achievements. Too often, those who have access to clean water in abundance take it for granted; to them, access to clean water is not a problem to be solved. When you become aware of others around you, however, who lead a very different life, without, for example, that assurance of clean water pouring from a tap, you:

◆ Identify same and different as you recognize how your life differs from that of others
◆ Create mental images of what it would be like if you faced the same challenges as others
◆ See multiple sides to a situation: yours and theirs
◆ Predict outcomes if the situation does not change.

These are some of the executive function skills that students use in the first step of a design process (Chapter 6), formulating the problem. You can't lead if you can't empathize.

Offer students opportunities to build the super-skill of empathy throughout the day. Engage them in solving real-world problems in the school, community, state, country, world, and beyond. Fourth-grade students research and make dog biscuits for the 11th Hour Rescue because the shelter needs food; they write grants for all other classrooms in the school to have flexible seating, because others found theirs to be so conducive to learning; they pitch the cafeteria director to include new, healthy foods. High school students design solutions to quelling civil wars around the world; they create pamphlets to build awareness of human trafficking. Middle school students create PSAs to promote healthy decisions; they design biodome possibilities for life on other planets. Connect students with current news, asking them to identify a challenge and consider how it affects others.

Teach students that the first step to resolving a conflict with a peer is to work to understand how the peer feels. If you use Peer Experts in the classroom, teach them that the first step to helping is to work to understand how the peer feels and what s/he is experiencing. If the day isn't working out the way you planned, be transparent and let your students know what you're experiencing and how you feel about it. Use every opportunity to build the leadership super-skill of empathy in your students.

Vision

Your vision is your "why!" It's the purpose that drives your actions and decisions. It's bigger than a goal, which is more about the "what?" Students in school should be formulating a vision for who they want to be, though that vision should obviously be open to maturation over the years. Offer vision-formulating questions, such as:

◆ Describe the person you would like to be when you grow to be an adult.
◆ How do you want other people to describe you?
◆ If you could change the school in any way, what would you want to accomplish?
◆ If you could change this country in any way, what would you want to accomplish?
◆ If you could change the world in any way, what would you want to accomplish?

A kindergarten classroom wall with the title "If I Were President" is filled with pictures of students dressed like a president with their vision for what they would accomplish. It's the beginning of a school career of defining their personal vision.

The key to visioning is to have a future-focused idea of who you want to be and what you want to accomplish. This requires a number of executive function skills, including: *changing perspective, holding onto information while considering other information, creativity,* and *creating mental images.*

Give students time to formulate a vision. At the youngest grades, focus them on their vision for themselves throughout the school year, keeping in mind that one's vision defines purpose. Help students move beyond, for example, "do my homework" to "learn all I can so I can help others" or "make myself proud."

Share with students the vision statements of well-known organizations, such as:

◆ Disney: "To make people happy"
◆ Habitat for Humanity: "A world where everyone has a decent place to live"
◆ Lego: "Inspire and develop the builders of tomorrow"
◆ Life is Good: "Spreading the power of optimism"
◆ Nike: "To bring inspiration and innovation to every athlete" ("If you have a body, you are an athlete.")
◆ Microsoft: "To help individuals and businesses realize their full potential"
◆ Pepsico: "Continually improve all aspects of the world in which we operate—environment, social, economic—creating a better tomorrow than today"

◆ San Diego Zoo: "To become a world leader at connecting people to wildlife and conservation"
◆ Uber: "Smarter transportation with fewer cars and greater access."

Encourage them to then write a vision statement of their own, helping them understand that a vision provides purpose to all your actions and goals.

Confidence

The poet e. e. cummings is credited with writing this line in a poem: "Once we believe in ourselves, we can risk curiosity, wonder, spontaneous delight or any experience that reveals the human spirit." Confidence fuels spontaneity, the willingness to risk failure, and happiness. It may seem like confidence comes from within, but you can foster confidence in students by capitalizing on a variety of executive function skills.

For many students, executive function skills are strengthening at home or through daycare centers and preschools before they begin kindergarten. Assuming they live in socially and emotionally healthy environments, these students may exhibit confidence. Students who enter school with deficits in executive function may be faced with an undesirable reality as they struggle to keep up with their peers, thus weakening their confidence. Addressing executive function deficits will help to bolster confidence. Depending on the confidence level of a student, start small and build up.

For example, as young students learn to *categorize* information, praise them for their success. Give them a set of images to *categorize* and ask if they believe they can *categorize* them. As they succeed, they will be building self-confidence: a belief in one's abilities and qualities.

Drawing on the executive function skill of *working towards a goal*, have students set a goal that is within reach, reflect on how difficult it will be to achieve, and acknowledge the achievement (see Table 7.1).

For older students, it is still useful to have them set a goal, reflect on their confidence level in achieving it, and then reflect again once they've accomplished it. Along the way, they will be strengthening the skill of *persisting in*

Table 7.1

My Goal	I think this will be:	I did it! I feel:
	❏ Easy ❏ Challenging ❏ Really Hard	

a task, among other executive function skills, as they work toward the goal. The deliberate focus on setting and achieving goals will increase student confidence.

It is important to guide students to set reasonable, attainable goals, even if, at first, you feel the goals are too easy. Achievement breeds confidence. Students may brag about being able to attain a goal that is outside of the realm of possibility. As they face the reality that they cannot attain that goal, their confidence will wane; you want to avoid this situation when working to build confidence.

As students work to build confidence, have them reflect, using a two-column page, on that in their lives for which they are grateful, and those accomplishments of which they are most proud (see Table 7.2).

As students build academic skills, provide them with the opportunities to be a Peer Expert or run a Small-Group Mini-Lesson. Ensure that students understand the target skill to the necessary level and can explain it to others. Setting students up to help others is another confidence booster.

Help students avoid being in situations that will diminish their confidence. As students strengthen their executive function skills of *self-assessing* and *considering future consequences of current action*, they will build a more accurate sense of their abilities and qualities and place themselves in situations in which they will succeed, thus growing their confidence as well as their abilities and qualities. A first-grade teacher offered students several books from which to choose, pointing out difficulty levels. A struggling reader came up to her after the group meeting and said he really wanted to read a particular book, that he knew it was harder than what he had been reading, but if she helped him, he knew he could do it. And so he did!

Table 7.2

I'm most grateful for …	*I'm most proud of …*

Courage

When you attempt to tackle that of which you are afraid, confronting your sense of fear and uncertainty, you demonstrate courage. Leaders are courageous. They do not crumble in the face of fear, failure, or uncertainty; they persist. This is not to say you should encourage students to persist no matter the cost; rather you should help them determine the source of their fear and help them to overcome reasonable fear.

The starting point for courage is identifying your core beliefs. What is "right" from your point of view? Students must make choices daily to overcome or resist situations related to bullying, lying, cheating, drugs, sex, and more. Their courage will rise from a strong sense of what they believe and the willingness to risk unpopularity for what they believe.

Young students may need courage to speak up in front of the class, to try a difficult task, to be friends with an unpopular student, and so forth. Be mindful of such situations and help students build courage. A reflective journal question or graphic organizer can help (see Table 7.3).

Building courage strengthens a variety of executive function skills, including: identifying cause and effect relationships, *seeing multiple sides to a situation, anticipating, evaluating, predicting outcomes, persisting in a task*, and *thinking before acting*.

Share stories of courageous leaders and have students discuss and write about what they believed and how they exhibited courage. In reading fiction, draw students' attention to characters that demonstrate courage and those who do not.

Courage is a leadership super-skill; there are many opportunities for students to focus on and build courage in their daily school lives. Look for those opportunities and capitalize on them.

Table 7.3

I am afraid of:	Because:
I overcame my fear by:	The result was:

Systems Thinking

If you came upon the parts of a bicycle lying in a heap, you'd potentially have trash: two wheels, gears and chain, handlebars, brakes, pedals. The pile of pieces would not serve any purpose. However, if you came across a bicycle, with all its component pieces in place, you would have a system that could enhance your life. You hop on and start pedaling and the bicycle moves; you turn the handlebars and you start moving in a new direction; you push backward on the pedal and it stops. When a collection of components work together to create a more complex object, you have a system.

The solar system consists of a sun at the center, with a tremendous pull of gravity that keeps planets in a path revolving around it. The planets in turn exert a gravitational pull that keeps smaller moons revolving around them. Other smaller, celestial bodies such as asteroids, comets, and meteors that are kept in orbit due to gravity are also part of the solar system. Individually, these components are simply planets, moons, the sun, and other celestial bodies. Together, they form the solar system. They have a relationship to one another. The moons revolve around planets; the planets revolve around the sun.

The English language is a system. Consider these words: bed, dog, barking, little, ate, retired, eventually, then, to, and, the, his. The list of words has no meaning. However, when you assign each word a role (noun, adjective, verb, adverb, preposition, conjunction, article, pronoun) and position them to interact with one another, you have meaning. For example: The barking dog eventually ate and then retired to his little bed.

Systems can also consist of actions, for example the system for a fire drill. All the actions that everyone takes to effectively complete a fire drill form together to make a system.

Systems can be made up of ideas. An economic system is the interrelationships among production, allocation, and distribution of goods and services among a group of people in a given geographic area. Capitalism, socialism, and communism are three types of economic systems.

When you think in terms of systems, you see a bigger picture, and you see relationships among the parts to create a more complex whole. You see how one aspect of a system affects another and what the impact would be if one part of the system were missing. Leaders must see systems and make decisions based upon systems, with the intent of creating and maintaining healthy and effective systems for all involved.

Let's return to the bicycle as an example. A simple bicycle consists of the components presented in Figure 7.2. Each of these components has a specific role in the working of a bicycle. However, no matter how effective or high-quality each component is, one component does not comprise a bicycle; it cannot perform its role alone.

Rotating the pedals causes the gears to turn, which causes the rear wheel to turn, which causes the front wheel to begin motion, thus moving the bicycle. The handle bars shift the direction of the front wheel, and thus steer the bicycle. Moving the pedals backward causes the brakes to engage, which causes the rear wheel to stop, which causes the front wheel to stop. Figure 7.3 illustrates some of the systems connections inherent in a bicycle.

In a systems diagram, you represent the components of a system as nodes, in this case circles. The relationship between two of the components is represented with a line. Figure 7.4 depicts the obvious relationships that exist.

Figure 7.2

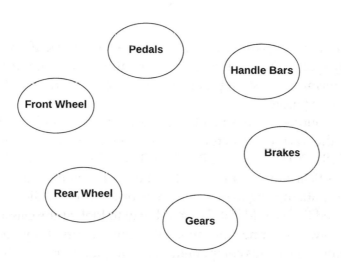

Figure 7.3

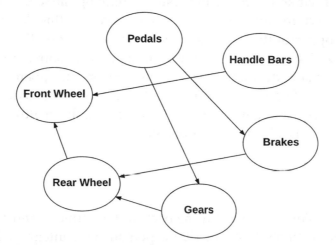

Figure 7.4

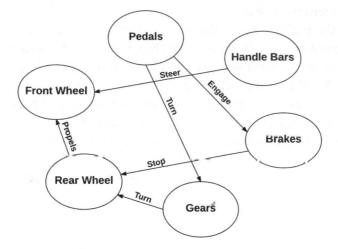

If those relationships are strong, the bicycle will work; if not, it won't. So it is with any system. You define the ideal relationships among components; then you determine the strength of each and work to improve the interrelationships where possible.

A team of fourth- grade students were going to help kindergarten students understand the various structures of the *Learner-Active, Technology-Infused Classroom* (Sulla, 2011), such as a Problem-Based Task, Analytic Rubric, Activity List, Help Board, and so forth. They began by listing the various structures and were attempting to put them in priority order. While facilitating, the teacher realized this would not be a good way to look at the classroom, so she asked if they saw any connection among the components. They said, "yes" and began drawing the various components as nodes, then drawing lines between the nodes. They started discussing how each pair of components depended on one another. Their ability to see the systems thinking made it easier for them to see the big picture and help lead others to success in this classroom.

Identify opportunities for students to draw systems diagrams in their learning for various systems, including perhaps, classroom helpers, community helpers, a plant, the human body, the solar system, a poem, an economic model, a system of equations, and so forth. Have them consider the interrelationships that exist among components, assessing the health of the system. Systems thinking is a leadership super-skill.

Integrity

Honest, responsible, trustworthy, respectful, fair, ethical, and true to one's word are the qualities that describe a person with integrity. People who will follow a leader need to trust that person to hold these qualities in high regard and demonstrate them consistently through their actions and words. Teachers help students build integrity by providing opportunities for them to reflect on and demonstrate these qualities.

Engage students in talking about the qualities of integrity, having them identify these qualities in characters in stories and novels and in famous people. Use pictures and quotes as openers for engaging students in discussions or written assignments related to integrity. Praise students when they demonstrate these qualities. When students fail to demonstrate these qualities, for example if they cheat on a test, steal from a peer, or act disrespectfully, go beyond punishment or consequences to have students reflect on and talk about the difference between their actions and integrity. In other words, create a culture of integrity in the classroom.

Intuition

Were you ever involved in a situation where you just knew what was going on, without having to think through it? Have you ever had a gut feeling about something? That's intuition; it's an inner-knowing. Intuition lets you see possibilities. While strong leaders certainly use data and reasoning, what sets them apart is that they have a strong sense of intuition that helps guide their decisions.

Intuition is cultivated over time based on processing experiences and being open to feeling through a situation rather than just reasoning through. Some of your students will be more naturally intuitive than others, based on their personality types. All students, however, can cultivate intuition, even if they are young and lack the breadth of experiences of adults.

In problem-solving situations, whether academic, social, or emotional, ask students to talk about what they feel their next step or action should be. Offer students opportunities to consider a scenario and offer their immediate sense of what they would do in the situation.

Have students look at pictures of people and describe what they think the person is like in reality. Using their observational skills to draw conclusions absent of any real data will help build intuitive skills.

Journal writing is good for building intuition because it causes you to reflect on situations, how you felt in advance, whether or not that proved out, and so forth. You might focus students on journaling about a subject area, problem-based task they're solving, their interactions with colleagues during collaboration, or life outside of school.

Summary for Demonstrating Leadership (#EF_Leadership)

Leadership skills can be considered the highest-level outcome of an educational system, when following conscious control, engagement, collaboration, empowerment, and efficacy. The super-skills of leadership are: confidence, courage, empathy, integrity, intuition, systems thinking, and vision. You can provide students with opportunities to build these super-skills in the classroom, which in turn will strengthen all the executive function skills.

◆ Empathy—the ability to put yourself in the place of another person to understand what that person is experiencing and feeling. There is no power differential in empathy. More powerful than sympathy, it is the spark that ignites great achievement.

◆ Vision—the purpose that drives your actions and decisions.

◆ Confidence—a belief in your abilities and qualities. It fuels spontaneity, the willingness to risk failure, and happiness.

◆ Courage—the willingness to stand up for your beliefs and to tackle that of which you are afraid.

◆ Systems Thinking—the ability to look at a whole, seeing many components and their interrelationships.

◆ Integrity—of possessing honesty, responsibility, trustworthiness, fairness, ethics, and a commitment to your word.

◆ Intuition—an inner knowing that guides decisions, letting you see possibilities.

References

Barker, J. A. (1992). *Paradigms: The business of discovering the future*. New York: Harper Collins.

Sulla, N. (2011). *Students taking charge: Inside the Learner-Active, Technology-Infused Classroom*. New York: Routledge.

8

Building Executive Function
Through Teacher Facilitation

I was sitting in a courtyard at an outdoor cafe. A man walked in with his young son and said to him, "Where do you want to sit?" The boy started walking to a table that had a cell phone and keys on it. The man said, "We can't sit there. Someone is sitting there." The boy kept staring at the table and the man followed with, "Someone's stuff is on the table, which means someone else is sitting there. We need to find an empty table. Where else do you want to sit?" The boy turned away from the table and scanned the other tables.

The interaction may seem innocent enough but it is filled with opportunities to build executive function. Think about it through the lens of executive function and the skills listed in Appendix A:

- "Where do you want to sit?" activates *shifting focus from one event to another*, *attending*, and *focusing*.
- "We can't sit there. Someone is sitting there." activates *managing conflicting thoughts* (where the boy wants to sit vs. the father saying they can't sit there).
- "Someone's stuff is on the table, which means someone else is sitting there." activates *identifying cause-and-effect relationships*.
- "We need to find an empty table. Where else do you want to sit?" activates *holding on to information while considering other information*, *working towards a goal*, and *persisting in a task*.

The rich opportunity to build executive function skills would not have occurred if the father had simply said, "Let's sit here," rather than allowing the boy to choose an appropriate place to sit. In this scenario, the man facilitated the boy's learning of how to select an appropriate place to sit.

As teachers work to design more student-centered, differentiated classrooms and reduce whole-class instruction, their roles must shift to actively facilitating learning. This creates the perfect venue for utilizing strategies that build executive function while focusing on academic skills.

The Power of Facilitation

Teacher facilitation of learning is the most powerful way to attain strong academic achievement for students. Days of "the lesson" must give way to days of powerful facilitation. With the advent of technology, students can access lessons on any content, watching countless videos of teachers, students, and field experts offering explanations of that content. Assuming students have the executive function skills to watch those lessons and make meaning from them, if the goal of school is for students to demonstrate awareness of content and present it on tests, we wouldn't need schools. New standards and today's society point to the need for students to understand content and, more so, demonstrate understanding of that content by applying it to new situations. Procedural automaticity is not enough; students must demonstrate novelty: "The ability to respond appropriately and successfully to novel situations" (Sulla, 2015, p. 9.) This level of understanding is best achieved by grappling with content, coupled with the masterful facilitation of teachers.

As you facilitate content mastery, you will be able to assess the executive function skill strengths and weaknesses of your students and offer instruction and guidance to match. For example, if a student has difficulty *focusing*, instead of saying, "look at the second sentence," you might use an index card to place under the sentence to which you are referring. If a student is conducting scientific experiments on plant growth using various nutrients but you assess s/he is weak in the executive function skill of analysis, you would not begin by looking at the graph and asking for the conclusion. You would ask questions to help the student build to a conclusion, for example:

- ◆ "Which bean plants had the most growth?"
- ◆ "What nutrient did you add to those while they were growing?"
- ◆ "Which bean plants had the least growth?"
- ◆ "What nutrient did you add to those while they were growing?"

If another student easily analyzes the data and draws conclusions, you might ask the student to propose a mix of nutrients and conduct another experiment to maximize growth based on existing data, which requires *making hypotheses, deductions, and inferences* as well as *anticipating* and *predicting outcomes*. Even though students are learning the same content, modify your facilitation based on individual student's executive function.

Preparing for Facilitation

As you move out of the role of content presenter to facilitator, you should first ensure your students have ample access to those content lessons you used to present from the front of the room. Provide students with access to a variety of texts, videos, learning centers, and other resources for instruction. Create a set of screencasts, podcasts, or videos of your important lessons. Then, create an activity list so that students learn what they need to learn along with the options for that learning.

Suppose you were engaging students in addressing the challenge of why the continent of Africa is so rich with natural resources (diamonds, gold, iron ore, uranium, etc.) while its people are among the poorest in the world. You would ensure that students have access to a variety of texts, videos, and assignments aimed at providing instruction and information. You would then be able to sit with students to assess their progress, help them interpret charts and graphs, suggest other data they may want to collect, pose thought-provoking questions, and more to advance individual learning. If your students have a motivating problem to solve and access to learning resources, they'll manage their time, freeing you up to facilitate their learning. You'll engage in more powerful and interesting discussions.

If you were engaging students in learning the power of different types of sentences, you would first ensure they had learning centers, How-To Sheets, videos, and texts that provided instruction. You would then be free to sit with individual students to assess learning, asking them, for example, to address the same point through different types of sentences or asking them to write a persuasive paragraph using varied types of sentences to build a case. You might ask a student to convert an exclamatory sentence into an interrogative sentence. You would not ask the same questions or make the same suggestions to all students; you would react to the student based on the information you glean.

Facets of Facilitation

Facilitation of learning is a complex skill that is highly dependent upon the learner, as not every learner needs the same coaching to succeed. Therefore, a good facilitator quickly assesses the situation and the learner's needs, and then offers assistance or asks questions based on that assessment. When you

Figure 8.1

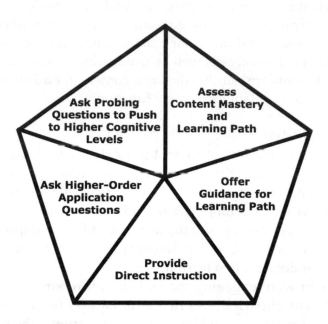

facilitate learning, your lens shifts from teaching to learning. Take a minute to consider that shift. If my focus is teaching, I start showing you how even if you're not ready or able to understand. If my focus is learning, I start by determining where you are in the learning process; I then offer guidance and instruction based on that information. If French were my native language and you were going to France, in need of some useful phrases, I could either start by speaking phrases and acting them out or by asking you if you already know any French words and finding out more about where you're going. Pronouncing the "r" sound in French can be challenging. If my focus were on teaching, I would teach you more about that; if my focus were on learning, I would listen to see if you need help with that skill before I taught it. The actions you take in facilitating learning are best summarized in the Facets of Facilitation graphic in Figure 8.1.

- ◆ **Assess Content Mastery and Learning Path:** Observe and ask questions to determine students' progress. One aspect of this facet is to ascertain students' progress related to content mastery; another is to assess their use of executive function in the learning process; and the third is to gain an understanding of the learning activities they are choosing to pursue content mastery.
- ◆ **Offer Guidance for Learning Path:** Based on your initial assessment, is the student engaging in appropriately leveled activities? Is the student focusing too much on one type of learning

(e.g., videos, peer experts, learning centers, etc.)? Determine what you think an appropriate next step would be and offer students guidance in their decision-making process for learning. You might suggest a resource. For example, for students who are studying the U. S. election process and are considering elections throughout history that were won despite the popular vote going to the opposing candidate, you might suggest they use the website www.270towin.com as a resource. For a student who shares a strong statement for or against the electoral college, you might suggest researching and creating a list of pros and cons.

◆ **Provide Direct Instruction:** At times, you'll provide direct instruction in the content. For example, if a student is struggling with two-digit addition with regrouping, you would demonstrate the skill, then guide the student through the process. You don't always want to go right to direct instruction; it may be more effective to help the student grapple with content by offering suggestions and guiding questions. However, there will be times when the student is either too frustrated or too lost, and the best option is to directly teach the content.

◆ **Ask Higher-Order Application Questions:** As you determine that students understand the content, ask questions that allow them to demonstrate application of the content in different situations. This will further solidify their understanding of the content. For example, if a student demonstrates understanding of the physics underlying the use of a fulcrum and lever to move an object, you might ask what it would take to lift a stack of books up to a table. If a student can explain the differences among types of communities (i.e., rural, suburban, and urban), you might ask how his/her own daily life would change in a different type of community. If students are learning about narrative techniques, such as the narrative hook, you could ask the student to give you a narrative hook to introduce a story about the past weekend.

◆ **Ask Probing Questions to Push to Higher Cognitive Levels:** As students continue to demonstrate mastery of content to the level of application, ask questions to push them to explore advanced application or content. If students build a roller coaster model that contains an initial drop, track, and one complete loop; and they construct it such that a marble maintains momentum and stays on track throughout; you might ask if they could incorporate a second loop. If a student is demonstrating mastery of the purpose and usage of compositional risks, you might ask if s/he can invent a new type of compositional risk. If students are counting with color rods, stacking up the ones, you might ask how they could use the rods to skip-count by twos. Consider the following question stems:

◆ "What if …?" Questions that begin with "what if" tend to push students to higher-order thinking. If they end with an open-ended scenario, they will boost creative thinking. For example, "What if we can't get the resources we need?" "What if the owls don't like our owl box?" "What if the book could end differently?"

◆ "What else …?" is a good way to move students beyond their current decision or solution. "What else could you do?" "What else could you use to accomplish this?" "What else could you add to this?"

◆ "Suppose …" can offer students an open-ended scenario. "Suppose you didn't have a ruler to solve this problem." "Suppose you had met Martin Luther King Jr." "Suppose you didn't have any paint and had to invent your own." "Suppose you were a character in this book." "Suppose there is ample water on Mars to support life." "Suppose we could clone a dinosaur to have here at our school." The idea is to keep offering slightly more difficult challenges to push students' learning to higher and higher levels.

During the facilitation process, it's important to remember that students don't know what they don't know; so, asking if they need help, and walking away if they don't, is not conducive to learning. Use the Facets of Facilitation to ensure you are moving students to a higher level of achievement. What you facilitate will be driven by your content; how you facilitate will be driven by students' executive function. You may need more concrete examples, graphic organizers, scaffolded questions, and so forth to compensate for lack of executive function, working to build those skills as well.

The Facilitation Roadmap

Even keeping in mind the Facets of Facilitation, how you respond to each student will also depend on the student's state of mind in the learning process. Learning is hard; grappling with new content is challenging. It's important to assess how students are feeling in the learning process to ensure your actions meet their needs. Figure 8.2 offers a snapshot of this process.

Figure 8.2

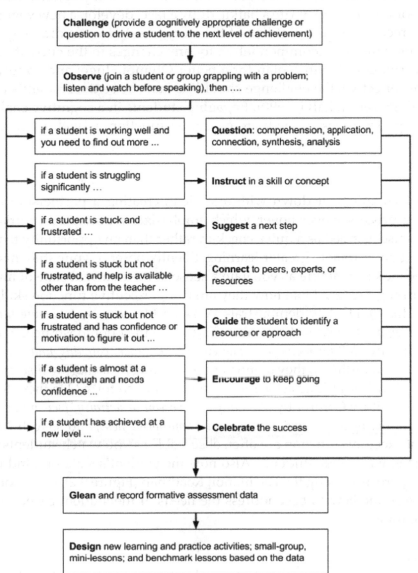

Challenge

True learning begins with a challenge that presents a level of cognitive dissonance: the gap between what the learner already knows and what is yet to be learned. The challenge causes the learner to grapple with content, working with it in a minds-on, and sometimes hands-on, fashion to construct meaning. The challenge can be focused on a small set of skills or encompass the application of a variety of skills: Make a collage of pictures of words that begin with the letter "b;" write a story using only words without the letter "e;" figure out what items you can purchase from the classroom store for $5; write a haiku; draw a face; develop a new vegetarian dinner recipe; create a plot line of the story; create a scale drawing of the classroom; make a recommendation for any changes to the current system of government; design a plan for a better Olympic luge; and so forth. To be most effective, the challenge should be just above the student's ability level (Csikszentmihalyi, 1990). Engaging students in a cognitive challenge offers opportunities to facilitate executive function as well as academic content.

Observe

When facilitating, sit down with a student, creating a partnership in the learning process. Never hover, which emphasizes a power differential and can be misconstrued as a quick check-in rather than an opportunity to probe thinking and promote greater learning. Silently observe your students for a few seconds to a minute as you gain a sense of their current state of mind in the learning process. Note how they are using executive function skills (see Appendix A). Do they demonstrate Working Memory by *following multiple steps, categorizing information*, and so forth? Do they demonstrate Cognitive Flexibility by *shifting focus from one event to another, catching and correcting errors*, and so forth? Do they demonstrate Planning by *managing time, working towards a goal, organizing actions and thoughts*, and so forth? Do they demonstrate Inhibitory Control by *attending to a person or activity, focusing, concentrating, initiating a task, maintaining social appropriateness*, and so forth? These areas of executive function are often observable as you watch students work or engage with other students. Also note the student's state of mind in the learning process. Using the Facilitation Roadmap (Figure 8.2) as a guide, you can determine how to best address the needs of the student based on that state of mind.

Question

If a student is working well and is not exhibiting frustration or boredom, you can find out more about her/his academic learning by asking questions. In the process, you'll pick up on executive function strengths and differences; however, your questions can also foster executive function. Consider the executive function skills in Appendix A and craft questions to help students reflect on executive function skills. Here is a set of question you might pose to a student:

◆ What are you working on? (*shifting focus from one event to another, attending to a person or activity*, and *remembering details*).

◆ How is it going? (*self-assessing, evaluating, organizing actions and thoughts*, and *holding on to information while considering other information*).

◆ How have you found help when you've needed it? (*defining a problem, generating possible solutions, maintaining social appropriateness*, and *thinking before acting*).

◆ What's your next step? (*remembering details, storing and manipulating visual and verbal information, monitoring performance*, and *reflecting on goals*).

Questions like these will help you assess your students' progress and state of mind while having them exercise executive function.

Instruct

If you note through observation or questioning that a student is struggling significantly, to the point of giving up, you need a fast, successful intervention. If you and your students engage in mindfulness training, you might suggest taking a few deep breaths before continuing. Then, provide direct instruction in the skill or concept so that the student gets the necessary information. At this point, attempting to walk a student through the skill by asking guiding questions might prove too frustrating. "Let me show you," could be a welcome statement. While offering the instruction, use deliberate language to demonstrate executive function skills. Deliberately point out any *cause-and-effect relationships*; *categorize information* using a table or simple drawing; if you are *following multiple steps*, number them, verbally or on paper; point out *multiple sides to a situation* as you address the skill or concept, and so forth. Make deliberate references to executive function skills.

Suggest

If a student is stuck and frustrated, but not at the point of giving up, you might suggest a next step. The student's state of mind might be too frustrated to offer suggestions for merely finding help; literally offer the next step in the cognitive process for grappling with the content. If a student is attempting to build words from letters and is stuck, you might offer a hint, or put two letters together, pronounce them, and ask what it sounds like. If a student is stuck getting started solving $3x + 5 = 17$, you might say "Okay, your goal is to get the variable x by itself on one side of the equal sign. So, the first step is to eliminate any numbers that are added or subtracted, in this case you have to subtract the 5 from the left." You can then wait to see if the student then continues to subtract 5 from the right or remains stuck. If a student is stuck identifying phrases in text that indicate transcendentalism, you might say, "So the key beliefs of transcendentalism are nonconformity, free thought, self-reliance, confidence, and nature. Let's see if we can identify any of those in this paragraph."

Use questions and statements, such as: "What if you …?"; "Okay, you've gotten this far, now you'll want to …"; "The next thing I would do is …"; then wait while the student takes that next step to see if you are still needed or if you've provided that key to having the student continue in the process without you. Making a suggestion can support *storing and manipulating visual and verbal information*, *following multiple steps*, *working towards a goal*, *organizing actions and thoughts*, *concentrating*, and *persisting in a task*.

Connect

If a student is stuck but not frustrated, you have the opportunity to build upon their resourcefulness by connecting the student with peers, experts, or resources. First ask if the student already asked anyone else for help or sought out resources. You might suggest a peer who could prove to be helpful or refer to an anchor chart hanging on the wall. If you know of a How-To Sheet or video that would offer step-by-step directions, share where to find that. You might have the student conduct a web search to locate information. Rather than offering the answer, you're offering a path to the answer. This helps support the executive function skills of *shifting focus from one event to another* (from being stuck to looking to obtain help), *holding onto information while considering other information* (the troubling aspect of the task and how to find help), and *thinking about multiple concepts simultaneously* (the various ways to locate help).

Guide

If a student is stuck but not frustrated and has the confidence and motivation to break through, you can guide the student to identify how they can approach the challenge. If you have structures in place for students to receive help (e.g., Help Board, Peer Expert Board, and Resource Area) you might start by asking, "When you're stuck, where can you look in the room for help?" You might remind them of processes they've used in the past, including guiding them to *apply former approaches to new situations*. "Remember when we …?" can trigger an idea for using a process. For example, if you taught a student to build rhyming words in a game by cycling through different beginning consonants (i.e., bat, cat, fat, hat, etc.), and the student is now stuck writing a poem, you can say, "Remember how we found words in that rhyming game?" That may be enough to trigger a solution for the student. It fosters *identifying same and different* (how one activity is similar to and different from another), *applying former approaches to new situations*, and *remembering details*.

Encourage

If a student is almost at a breakthrough and needs confidence, offer words of encouragement to strengthen grit! Share your sense that the student is almost there. Explain how you like his/her persistence or the way s/he is working through the challenge. If the student is using drawings or models to help solidify thinking, explain how that's a great way to visualize the situation more concretely. Specifically name any executive function skills you see in action to draw the student's attention to progress in that area, such as, "I like how you're focusing on this and not letting anything distract you;" "I like how you are anticipating what might go wrong with this solution." You probably don't need to offer any tips for mastering the content; just strengthen the student's confidence.

Celebrate

If a student has achieved a new level of mastery, offer words of celebration! Avoid telling students they are "smart" and instead talk about what a great job they did and how proud you are of their effort (Dweck, 2006). Offer specific feedback about the work they produced, such as, "I like the way you ..." or "I'm particularly impressed with ..." and describe an aspect of the final product or performance. To strengthen executive function skills, ask students to share their goals for the work and reflect on how well they met them. Provide some metacognitive questions, such as, "How did you overcome any obstacles or challenges along the way?"

Glean

Through facilitation, you will glean a great deal of formative assessment data. Consider that quizzes and tests are focused on ensuring that everyone has mastered specific content by a specific time. Facilitation data is more organic and personal. During a conversation with one of your English as a New Language (ENL) students, you might realize that she is correctly using the simple past and past continuous tenses of verbs and understands the difference between them. You should capture that somewhere. In your algebra I class, during facilitation you realize a student has mastered solving linear equations with one variable but is struggling with solving systems of equations. You share that he should attend the Small-Group Mini-Lesson occurring in 10 minutes and direct him to work on another skill until then. You should capture that somewhere. A Content Facilitation Grid allows you to capture formative assessment data as it presents itself. The grid (see Table 8.1) consists of student names down the left side and content skills and concepts across the top.

Table 8.1 Medusa's Myth *Content Facilitation Grid*

Student	Identifies the elements of a myth	Describes lessons explained in a myth	Understands the concept of relevancy	Identifies relevant lessons for today	Identifies current examples of myths	Compares and contrasts lessons from ancient and modern myths	Understands setting and the effect on a story	Understands plot; that a story has a climax with rising actions and falling actions	Understands that writing has a clear climax with rising and falling actions	Maintains correct verb tense throughout a writing piece	Uses figurative language	Describes how a particular story or drama's plot unfolds	Determines a theme or central idea of a text	Analyzes the impact of specific word choices on meaning and tone	Describes how the characters respond or change as the plot moves toward a resolution	Uses standard English conventions accurately

As you facilitate, carry the grid and enter codes to indicate level of mastery, for example:

◆ M—mastery
◆ PT—can explain the skill or concept well enough to be a peer tutor
◆ HW—could use some reinforcement activities for homework
◆ ML—needs a Small-Group Mini-Lesson.

You could also create a separate facilitation grid for executive function skills with codes representing level of attainment, for example:

◆ NE—not evident
◆ PR—preliminary awareness and execution with prompting
◆ IN—initial level of execution without prompting
◆ AT—attainment: consistent execution.

Design

Based on the data on student learning that you glean during facilitation, along with quizzes and graded assignments, you can design future learning opportunities. They might include whole-group Benchmark Lessons, Small-Group Mini-Lessons, Learning Centers, How-To Sheets, screencasts, and more. As you analyze your Content Facilitation Grid, looking across will let you know how individuals are faring. As you design learning activities, consider individual students' executive function skills so that you can design appropriate supports for content learning. As you look vertically at your Content Facilitation Grid, you'll get a sense of how effective your instructional plan is and where you may need additional Learning Activities for content that most students are not mastering.

Make Your Thinking Transparent

As you approach your content and assist students in building mastery, consider how you mastered it and how you navigated your way through the challenges. Walk students through that as you facilitate; guide them in grappling with content. Rather than saying, "First you do this ..." share how you would go about solving the problem by saying, "First I would wonder ..." or "First I would look to see if ..." For example, suppose a student is having trouble understanding character traits. Make your thinking transparent by saying, "So first I think, what is he like? What words might describe his personality? I think about his actions and what that might tell me. What did he do in the story? ... Yes, he kept giving away his toys and possessions to others who were in need. So, I think about what that tells me about him. What do you think? ... I figure he must be generous, and that's a word that would describe what he's like; generous would be one of his traits. Do you agree?"

Making thinking transparent is particularly important when teaching students reading of informational text across the content areas. While at first glance it might make sense for the language arts teacher to instruct students in reading, in fact the experience will be more rich and robust if content area teachers make their thinking transparent. When reading informational text, you engage in an internal conversation. You acknowledge what you already know; you ask questions that may or may not be answered as you continue to read. You make connections to other content you know. If you are a secondary subject-area teacher, you read informational text better than any teacher outside your subject because of your frame of reference. Now, as your students are working through informational text, make your internal conversations transparent to them.

Consider some content that you will be teaching. How would you work through it? How would you go about learning it? What questions would you ask yourself? How would you *categorize information*? What *cause-and-effect relationships* would you identify? What self-talk would you use to *persist in a task*? Make all that transparent to students.

Summary for Building Executive Function Through Teacher Facilitation

Facilitation is a necessary and powerful tool for ensuring student achievement. Use the Facets of Facilitation and the Facilitation Roadmap to guide you.

- ◆ Facets of Facilitation
    - ◆ Assess content mastery and learning path
    - ◆ Offer guidance for learning path
    - ◆ Provide direct instruction
    - ◆ Ask higher-order application questions
    - ◆ Ask probing questions to push to higher cognitive levels.

- ◆ Facilitation Roadmap
    - ◆ Challenge
    - ◆ Observe
    - ◆ Question
    - ◆ Instruct
    - ◆ Suggest
    - ◆ Connect
    - ◆ Guide
    - ◆ Encourage
    - ◆ Celebrate
    - ◆ Glean
    - ◆ Design

References

Csikszentmihalyi, M. (1990). *Flow: The psychology of optimal experience*. London: Harper Perennial.

Dweck, C. S. (2006). *Mindset: The new psychology of success*. New York: Random House.

Sulla, N. (2015). *It's not what you teach but how: 7 insights to making the CCSS work for you*. Routledge: New York.

9

Not a Course, But a Culture

Increasing executive function skills involves activating and accelerating brain development. Executive function is not a set of discrete skills to be mastered in a vacuum; it does not lend itself to becoming a course of study. Much like building fine-motor skills, through ongoing, embedded practice; that's how the brain solidifies executive function skills. That's not to say activities and games aimed at building executive function are not necessary; they just are not sufficient to truly making a difference. More than a course in school, make executive function skill development a culture reinforced by everyone in the school, and not just teachers, but every adult who encounters children: secretaries, custodians, aides, security guards, and so forth. Everyone can find a few executive function skills that can be addressed through their roles.

Given executive function skills are controlled by the prefrontal cortex of the brain, a key to improving executive function is to grow the brain! As with muscle growth, athletic prowess, and musical performances, practice makes perfect! The more you exercise the brain, the more it will grow. The key to exercising the prefrontal cortex is to include the use of executive function skills repeatedly throughout the day, thus infusing them into your students' daily activities, supporting them through classroom structures, and focusing on them during facilitation of learning.

Chapters 2 through 7 offered specific activities and structures for building executive function; Chapter 8 offered teacher facilitation strategies; this chapter will offer overall ideas for building a culture of executive function focus. The ideas that follow will help all students, however, they will be particularly beneficial to those who exhibit executive function deficits.

So, a first step in building executive function is to stimulate the body's natural ability to reduce stress, burn up excess cortisol produced by stress, and produce a reasonable amount of neurotransmitter chemicals in order to increase brain activity in the prefrontal cortex. The study of the prefrontal cortex related to growth and repair is relatively new, however, preliminary studies point to many situations that stimulate the prefrontal cortex. None should be considered a cure-all; and all should be implemented in moderation. Remember, too much of a good thing can turn out to be bad. Following are my suggestions for overall prefrontal cortex stimulation.

Get Students Moving!

Exercise increases blood flow and oxygen to the brain and has been shown to increase achievement (Hillman et al., 2009). Moderate exercise increases dopamine production and reduces cortisol in the bloodstream. So, if you can get your students moving every day, you can support the growth of the prefrontal cortex. However, intense workouts and endurance training can actually increase levels of dopamine to an unhealthy level. The key is to engage students in some level of regular movement. This is obviously easier to accomplish with younger students who can engage in regular exercise and movement sessions in class. You can build an exercise "brain break" into the day and have students exercise for 10–15 minutes in the morning and afternoon.

Get students moving while they practice, for example, automaticity of math facts or sight words. Have students practice memory skills, such as math facts or vocabulary, while running in place or performing jumping jacks. The exercise will increase blood flow and oxygen to the brain. Engaging in the cognitive task while moving will require students to *focus* and *concentrate* more than when seated. These exercise breaks can also be used with older students with significant executive function deficits. Research involving brain scans on students who sat for 20 minutes versus those who walked for 20 minutes showed a significant increase in brain activity for those who exercised, leading to higher test scores when walking just prior to a test.

For older students with typical or slightly lagging executive function skills, you might explain the importance of movement and have them commit to exercise 20–30 minutes a day for four days a week. If they exhibit enough executive function to be able to set goals and follow through, you can engage them in a personal, moderate exercise program.

For students of all ages, you can create an exercise chart that they are responsible for filling in as they engage in various sorts of exercises. Encourage students, too, to get involved in a sport or movement hobby of their liking.

The *Learner-Active, Technology-Infused Classroom* (Sulla, 2011) is an environment in which students regularly leave their seats and move around the room: switching from one activity to the next, which may involve joining another student or group, or moving to another location; moving to join a Small-Group Mini-Lesson; walking to the Resource Area to gather necessary materials for learning; etc. It is natural to see students walking around the classroom. While it would not be considered exercise, just taking some steps now and then is a start to activating the brain.

Whatever your classroom structure, include movement as part of your classroom routine. It may be as simple as asking students to stop and engage in ten jumping jacks or run in place. It may be asking students to stand in a group and discuss the topic of the day. A little exercise goes a long way when it comes to supplying oxygen to the brain and activating your prefrontal cortex.

Do you have students on the cross-country team? Suggest they mentally study for their next test while running after school.

Get Students Standing!

While schools are beginning to utilize stand-biased desks at which students can stand and work as a way of combating sedentary behavior and obesity, recent findings indicate positive effects on executive function. A study by Mehta et al. (2016) noted that "continued utilization of the stand-biased desks was associated with significant improvements in executive function and working memory capabilities" (p. 7). Standing for long periods of time can be problematic for the back; giving students options for standing and sitting will allow them to decide what works best for them.

Even if you don't have standing desks for students, get them standing while they talk about content with one another.

Close Those Eyes!

Have students stand with their eyes closed. This could be paired with listening to the teacher or a colleague share ideas or read aloud; it could be paired with reciting information to be memorized, such as automaticity of facts. Research studies have shown that the prefrontal cortex is activated when people close their eyes, and, more so, if they close their eyes while standing (Ouchi et al., 1999).

As part of an exercise cool-down, students could stand on two feet, one foot, and in tandem (one foot in front of the other), all with their eyes closed.

A brief closed-eye activity like this could activate the prefrontal cortex before or during engaging in academic work.

Get Students Laughing!

Jokes activate the prefrontal cortex, especially as they are delivered. The unexpected nature of a joke, for example, "knock, knock," spurs the prefrontal cortex into action as the brain attempts to make sense of it. "Who's there?" "Canoe" "Canoe who?" At this point, the prefrontal cortex is attempting to guess the punchline, with a mental image of a canoe. "Canoe come out and play?" Now the prefrontal cortex is resolving the incongruity; if it thinks the joke was funny, it will stimulate the pleasure center of the brain to smile and perhaps laugh. Smiling and laughter produces dopamine. I bet you never knew a joke could create such a complex set of actions in the brain. Build joke-telling into your students' day.

Similarly, context-based humor used in delivering content is very effective in students' retention of information. It's important that the joke or humor you use is related to the content and just humorous enough to elicit a giggle. Over-the-top jokes that start students bellowing actually have a negative effect on retention.

Keep a Gratitude Journal

Feeling gratitude activates the prefrontal cortex (Zahn et al., 2009). So, stop waiting for Thanksgiving! Have students keep a gratitude journal and write daily about that for which they are thankful. They can generate lists, draw pictures, or write journal entries. They can then share their thoughts with classmates.

Just saying the word, "thank you," from the heart, activates the prefrontal cortex. Prime your students to think about the various acts of kindness they offer and encounter during the day to build a more grateful classroom and student body.

Engage in Mindfulness Meditation

Take a minute to pay attention to your breathing. Can you feel and/or hear yourself inhaling and then exhaling? What happens to your body as you inhale and exhale? Pay attention to it. Take a few deep breaths while paying attention to them. Now resume normal breathing and pay attention to the changes in sound and body movement.

You've just engaged in a few minutes of mindfulness meditation (discussed briefly in Chapter 6), which has been proven to enhance brain function. If you meditate for as little as 15 minutes a day, after about two weeks you will begin to feel the effects on your body. Mindfulness meditation is somewhat easier than what people think of as traditional meditation in which you "switch off" your mind because you have something on which to focus, in this case, your breathing. While a few deep breaths will reduce anxiety, regular meditation begins to shrink the part of the brain that handles the fight or flight response and increase the prefrontal cortex, making you calmer overall and able to see "the big picture" in life.

Middle schools and high schools should consider a meditation program as part of the school day. For younger students, building in some mindfulness time can help with those test scores. Begin small, with a minute of guided mindfulness training where you talk students through focusing on their breathing, much as I did in the first paragraph of this section. Engage students for just a minute. Over time, build up to 5 minutes. You can find many resources for mindfulness meditation activities for young children on the Internet.

Look at Baby Animals

It turns out that looking at pictures of cute baby animals causes the brain to release dopamine and stimulates the prefrontal cortex. Luckily, the Internet is filled with cute baby animal videos. Include pictures of cute baby animals in your room design.

Get a Hobby!

Hobbies are known to boost *creativity* and, thus, dopamine. They are also good for exercising many executive function skills. Many hobbies can easily be included in the school day, and with encouragement, students might continue them at home. Some hobbies include scrapbooking, writing, and collecting (cards, shells, fruit and vegetable stickers, etc.). For younger students, have them build hobby time into their day. For older students, encourage them to pursue a hobby and offer them time to share monthly with one another in class.

Put the Music On!

Music stimulates the prefrontal cortex. Play music as students are entering and leaving school. For middle and high schools, play music as students change classes. Mellow, instrumental background music can be used in class. Remember that for some students, music can be a distraction, so it's best not to play it continuously.

Throw a Watermelon Party!

Certain foods work in the body to naturally boost dopamine; watermelon is one such food. Others that are appropriate for school include apples, bananas, dark chocolate, and pumpkin seeds. When you're planning events, snacks, and food-related activities, consider building these into the menu. You can also alert parents to snacks that will help boost their children's executive function. Search the Internet for complete lists of foods that are known to feed the prefrontal cortex and boost dopamine.

From the Classroom

I recently watched a video of primary level students, each with a large piece of paper on a wall, just painting away lines, squiggles, and other abstract brushstrokes while dancing to the music of Pharrell's song, "Happy." I thought, "What a great way to have students decorate the room!" This could happen at any grade level, with obvious adjustments for age. You would be building in movement, music, *creativity*—all dopamine boosters!

Years ago, an urban middle school principal with whom I consulted hosted a monthly breakfast gathering for students who had achieved 100% attendance in the past month. Part of the fun was singing Brenda Russell's song, "Get Here." In case you don't know the lyrics, here you go: "You can reach me by railway, you can reach me by trailway … I don't care how you get here, just get here if you can." The gathering ended with the students dancing the Macarena. Little did she know at the time that she had a veritable trifecta for increasing executive function:

◆ Effort-based results
◆ Music
◆ Movement.

Summary for Not a Course, But a Culture

Executive function is not a subject to be taught in a course; it's a set of skills connected to brain development that is best addressed by creating a culture of executive function:

- ◆ Get students moving
- ◆ Get students standing
- ◆ Close those eyes
- ◆ Get students laughing
- ◆ Keep a gratitude journal
- ◆ Engage in mindfulness meditation
- ◆ Look at baby animals
- ◆ Get a hobby
- ◆ Put the music on
- ◆ Throw a watermelon party

References

Hillman, C. H., Pontifex, M. B., Fernhall, B., Thompson, K. M., Valentini, T. A. (2009). The effect of acute treadmill walking on cognitive control and academic achievement in pre-adolescent children. *Neuroscience.* 159(3): 1044–1054.

Mehta, R., Shortz, A. E., Benden, M. E. (2016). Standing up for learning: A pilot investigation on the neurocognitive benefits of stand-biased school desks. *International Journal of Environmental Research and Public Health.* 13(1), 59; doi:10.3390/ijerph13010059

Ouchi, Y., Okada, H., Yoshikawa, E., Nobezawa, S., Futatsubashi, M. (1999). Brain activation during maintenance of standing postures in humans. *Brain.* Feb;122 (Pt 2) 329–338.

Sulla, N. (2011). *Students taking charge: Inside the Learner-Active, Technology-Infused Classroom.* New York: Routledge.

Zahn, R., Moll, J., Paiva, M., Garrido, G., Krueger, F., Huey, E. D., Grafman, J. (2009). The neural basis of human social values: Evidence from functional MRI. *Cereb Cortex*, 19(2): 276–283. doi: 10.1093/cercor/bhn080

Continuing the Conversation

I hope this book has left you with inspiration and ideas for helping all students succeed at high levels and develop into efficacious leaders. I hope, too, that closing the cover doesn't end our conversation and engagement. There are a variety of ways you can continue to engage with me and with others who have read the book:

- Use the Twitter hashtags to build a virtual conversation: #EF_ConsciousControl; #EF_Engagement; #EF_Collaboration; #EF_Empowerment; #EF_Efficacy; and #EF_Leadership.
- Visit IDE Corp. (www.idecorp.com) to locate my blog.
- Join a Virtual Learning Community (VLC) course on executive function or related topics (you'll find more at www.idecorp.com).
- Join the #LATICchat Twitter chat

Change the world!

Appendix A
Executive Function Skills

Working Memory Storing and manipulating visual and verbal information Identifying same and different Remembering details Following multiple steps Holding on to information while considering other information Identifying cause-and-effect relationships Categorizing information	**Problem Solving** Defining a problem Analyzing Creating mental images Generating possible solutions Anticipating Predicting outcomes Evaluating
Cognitive Flexibility Shifting focus from one event to another Changing perspective Seeing multiple sides to a situation Being open to others' points of view Being creative Catching and correcting errors Thinking about multiple concepts simultaneously	**Inhibitory Control** Attending to a person or activity Focusing Concentrating Thinking before acting Initiating a task Persisting in a task Maintaining social appropriateness
Planning Setting goals Managing time Working towards a goal Organizing actions and thoughts Considering future consequences in light of current action	**Self Awareness** Self-assessing Overcoming temptation Monitoring performance Reflecting on goals Managing conflicting thoughts
Reasoning Making hypotheses, deductions, and inferences Applying former approaches to new situations	

Appendix B
Group Discussion Protocol #5

Groups pose or are given questions to discuss based on texts, research, and ALU[1]– related activities. They then follow this protocol to engage in the discussion.

1. Prior to scheduling your group discussion, ensure that each member has received a "discussion pass" from the teacher.
2. Find a place to meet, ensuring that all members can sit comfortably and hear one another.
3. Select a *TimeKeeper*, a *BirdWalk Watcher*, a *Protocol Promoter*, and a *Materials Person*.
4. Use the "Placemat Activity" to individually write down key thoughts from your notes about the question you are discussing. The *TimeKeeper* should allow 5 minutes for the group to do so.
5. Begin a discussion using the following guidelines:
   a. Everyone listens to the speaker. No one starts searching for information for their next statement until a person finishes speaking.
   b. Acknowledge what others say with supportive or challenging comments, never with judgmental comments.
   c. Each new comment is presented to relate to prior comments or introduce a new idea that will further the conversation (as opposed to simply dropping a conversation thread.)
   d. Be mindful of who is speaking and ask those who have not spoken in a while to offer their opinions.
   e. To ensure you are seeing all sides of a situation, use the *Six Hats* protocol.
6. If part of your discussion is to arrive at a decision, use the *PMI* protocol to help. Ensure that all members can "live with" the decision.

Note

1 ALU – Authentic Learning Unit: A unit of study in a *Learner-Active, Technology-Infused Classroom* that has, at its core, an authentic, open-ended, problem for students to solve.

Appendix C

Effective Discussions: Brainstorming Protocol

Question or Problem: _____

Group Members: _____

1. You will need a *Reader, Recorder, TimeKeeper,* and *Encourager.* If you have fewer than four group members, double-up the roles as needed.
2. The *Reader* will read these directions to the group to guide the brainstorming process.
3. The *Recorder* will fill in the top two lines at the top of this page.
4. The *TimeKeeper* will keep track of the time to help keep the group on task.
5. Individually, spend 5 minutes thinking of ideas to address the question or problem. Don't judge any ideas; just keep generating.
6. The *Encourager* will go around the group, asking each person to offer one idea. No one is to comment on the ideas, positively or negatively. Keep going around; generate as many ideas as possible. The *Recorder* will write the ideas down so that everyone can see them. Spend at least 10 minutes generating ideas, more if you need it.
7. After the initial brainstorming, the *Reader* will read each of the ideas on the list, one at a time, while the *Encourager* asks group members to rank an idea from A (strongest) to C (weakest) in terms of:

   a. Applicability—How well does the idea address the question or problem?
   b. Feasibility—How likely is this idea to happen? Is it affordable? Is it possible?
   c. Interest—How interesting is the idea to you as a possibility?

   The *Recorder* will write down the A, B, C responses for A(ccountability), F(easibility), and I(nterest) next to each item.
8. The *Reader* will draw group members' attention to the list and ask everyone, based on the feedback, to select the top 3 ideas. The *Recorder* will circle each group member's top 3.

9. If there are more than 5 items circled, the *Reader* will ask the group members to pick the top two from the circled list. The *Recorder* will check off each group member's top 2 and cross out the rest.

10. If there are more than 5 items circled, the *Reader* will repeat the process, asking for just the top pick from the new list.

11. The *Encourager* should ask each group member to sign the paper with the ideas on it to state that the group adhered to the process and they agree with the list.

12. The group now has a small number of ideas to consider and research.

Appendix D

Listen and Draw

Complete this activity with one other person. Each of you will take turns creating a drawing and then telling the other how to draw it without showing it to them. Continue to take turns for the time period you have available to you.

1. Working alone where your partner cannot see what you're drawing, create a simple drawing. It may include:

    a. A square
    b. An equilateral triangle attached to the outside of the square
    c. An equilateral triangle attached to one or more inside lines of the square
    d. A circle attached to the outside of the square
    e. A circle attached to one or more inside lines of the square

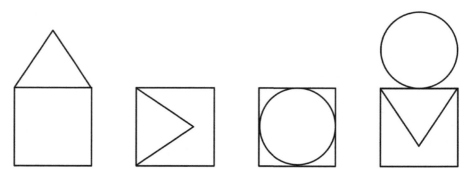

    Here are some examples:

2. Place your drawing inside a manila file folder.
3. Get a second manila folder and place a sheet of blank paper in it.
4. Find your partner and sit at a desk or table across from one another.
5. One of you will start as the *Direction Giver*, the other as the *Drawing Partner*.
6. The *Direction Giver* will place the manila folder with the drawing inside on the desk with the folded edge facing the *Drawing Partner*.
7. The *Drawing Partner* will place the manila folder with blank paper inside on the desk with the folded edge facing the Direction Giver.

© 2018 *Building Executive Function: The Missing Link to Student Achievement*, Nancy Sulla, Taylor & Francis

8. The *Direction Giver* will open the folder so that it creates a barrier to prevent the *Drawing Partner* from seeing the drawing.

9. The *Drawing Partner* will open the folder so that it creates a barrier to prevent the *Direction Giver* from seeing the blank sheet.

10. The *Direction Giver* will use only words to give the *Drawing Partner* directions to draw the figure. The *Direction Giver* may not look at what the *Drawing Partner* is drawing, and the *Drawing Partner* may only ask for the *Direction Giver* to repeat a direction, not clarify it.

11. When the drawing is complete, both partners reveal their drawings and reflect. The goal is not to criticize one another, but to get better at drawing from one another's directions. So discuss these questions to see how you might improve for the next drawing.

    a. How accurate was the drawing?
    b. Which directions were the most clear?
    c. Which directions might need to be changed to make it more clear?
    d. How well did the *Drawing Partner* follow the directions?

12. Switch roles and follow the directions from #6.

13. When you have finished both drawings, you may start again with a new set of drawings. Work on improving your ability to give and follow the directions for drawing the figure.

Appendix E

Great Student Rubric: Version 1

	Learning	Practicing	Got it!
I'm Ready to Learn	• I bring work, books, pencils or other tools when reminded. • I get to work when told.	• I come to class with all tools needed to learn. • I get my work done right away without being told.	All of Practicing plus I check the board for any changes or information from the teacher before getting to work.
I'm Responsible	• I complete most work on time. • I find a safe place to store my papers and other items so I don't lose them.	• I complete all my work on time. • I know where all my papers and belongings are. • I meet all deadlines.	All of Practicing plus when finished early, I spend time improving my work before handing it in.
I Pay Attention	• I usually stay on task. • I quickly get back on task with a reminder from teachers or classmates.	• I stay on task. • I quickly get back on task when distracted. • I keep off-task conversations for lunch or free time.	All of Practicing plus I take steps to stay focused, including moving to a better workspace to reduce distractions.
I Can Work with Others	• I carry out my role with reminders. • I sometimes share my materials and space.	• I work with my team to decide on roles and jobs. • I carry out my role effectively. • I share material and space.	All of Practicing plus I make sure that all group members have opportunities at all roles, materials, and classroom spaces.
I Manage My Time	• I plan my schedule with help. • I stick to my schedule with reminders. • I explain why some activities took longer or shorter.	• I plan my schedule without help. • I complete activities within the time limits. • I adjust my plan as needed while still meeting expectations.	All of Practicing plus I explain my strategies for planning and scheduling to others.

From www.ideportal.com © 2010–2015, IDE Corp.

© 2018 *Building Executive Function: The Missing Link to Student Achievement,*
Nancy Sulla, Taylor & Francis

Appendix F
Great Student Rubric: Version 2

	Novice	Apprentice	Practitioner	Expert *All of Practitioner plus*
Individual Responsibility	comes to class ready to learn: • brings completed homework • has materials and necessary tools • with prompting, starts tasks	• starts tasks without prompting from teacher • uses the "Help Board" rather than interrupting the teacher • completes activities for group work	• Completes all work to be handed in on time when in need of help: • re-reads directions • reviews notes • quietly asks others for help • adds name to "Help Board" • if unable to continue, moves on to something else productive	When finished early, spends time improving the work to be handed in or works on challenge or optional activities
Folder Organization	• brings any current and prior work needed for class each day	• organizes work for easy access using "in progress" and "completed" pockets	• stores current schedule and activity list, direction sheets, current unfinished work, and completed work for the unit in ways that allow easy access • stores papers from previous units at home	able to explain organization strategy and changes made over time
Focus	• with prompting from teacher or peer, starts tasks • if off task, with prompting from teacher or peer, resumes task	• recognizes loss of focus and gets back on task • when working individually, chooses a seat to minimize distractions	• stays on task throughout an activity • switches from one activity to the next with minimal "down time" • refrains from distracting others • reserves off-task conversations for out-of-class time	explains strategies for Effectively staying focused during school and homework
Participation	participates in group lessons and activities	• comes to group lessons and activities prepared • asks and answers questions to clarify content or directions • offers ideas	• follows through on all group responsibilities • actively listens to others and relates comments to their contributions • uses text to back up opinions • asks higher-order, content-related questions	• offers praise and constructive criticism to peers • accepts and utilizes constructive criticism

From www.ideportal.com © 2010–2015, IDE Corp.

Appendix G

Great Student Rubric: Version 3

This rubric was inspired by Paul Tough's book, *How Students Succeed*, and the character program at the Kipp School in NYC.

	Novice begin reflecting here	Apprentice	Practitioner read here first	Expert all of Practitioner plus
Grit and Optimism	• sets clear goals • identifies skills and topics that are a struggle and believes growth is possible	• perseveres with even difficult tasks • when struggling, identifies reasons behind failure and tries new strategies	• consistently hands in quality work on time • persists through challenges to achieve quality work • analyzes failures and setbacks and develops strategy for breaking through	• articulates strategies to develop grit • explains how optimism affects success in class
Self-Control	• brings prior work necessary for class each day • gets to work with reminders • when off-task, returns to task when prompted	• gets to work right away without reminders • maintains appropriate volume in class • identifies at least two strategies to stay focused in class • has responses for distraction • uses directions to increase success	• uses rubric to help guide learning throughout the unit • accurately self-checks work in class • uses directions and notes to help answer questions before asking others • refrains from distracting others • refrains from interrupting others when speaking	• explains organizational strategies and changes made over time • explains the strategies used for effectively managing time in school and at home
Collaboration: Gratitude and Social Intelligence	• identifies a clear role during partner or small group work • is polite to peers (including *please* and *thank-you*) • is polite to teacher (including *please* and *thank-you*) • keeps temper in check	• adapts to different social situations • allows others to speak without interruption (actively listens) • follows through on partner or small group responsibilities • helps group meet goals • works to resolve differences with others	• able to find solutions to conflicting opinions with others • shows appreciation • puts forth effort to make a difference for others in class • makes suggestions to group to work more effectively	• assists group members in reaching consensus and resolving conflict

(continued)

	Novice begin reflecting here	Apprentice	Practitioner read here first	Expert all of Practitioner plus
Curiosity and Zest	• identifies topics in class that are interesting/ exciting to explore	• demonstrates enthusiasm for learning and applying content	• asks questions to aid in learning more effectively • approaches new situations with excitement and energy	• makes real world connections to content from class without prompting

From www.ideportal.com © 2010–2015, IDE Corp.

Appendix H
Using a Venn Diagram

A Venn Diagram lets you think about two things and see how they are alike and how they are different. Let's try it with a cat and a dog.

☐ 1. On your paper, draw two big circles that overlap in the middle, like this:

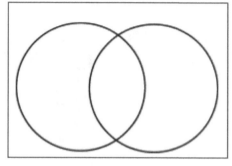

☐ 2. Over the left circle, write the word cat, like this:

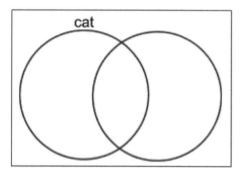

☐ 3. Over the right circle, write the word dog, like this:

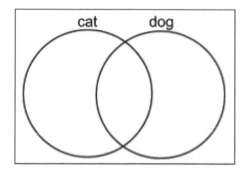

☐ 4. Think about a cat and a dog. How are they alike? Write some ideas on the inside where the two circles overlap, like this:

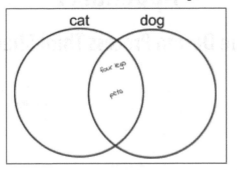

☐ 5. See if you can find five ways in which a cat and dog are alike.

☐ 6. Now think about how a cat is different from a dog. Write some ideas on the left side, under cat, but not in the middle of the two circles.

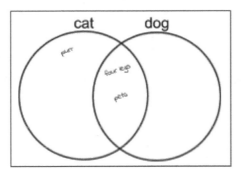

☐ 7. See if you can find four ways a cat is different from a dog.

☐ 8. Now think about how a dog is different from a cat. Write some ideas on the right side, under dog, but not in the middle of the two circles.

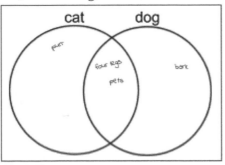

☐ 9. See if you can find four ways a cat is different from a dog.

10. When you are done you'll have a diagram of similarities and differences. That's what a Venn diagram is good for!

Appendix I
The Design Process ThinkSheet

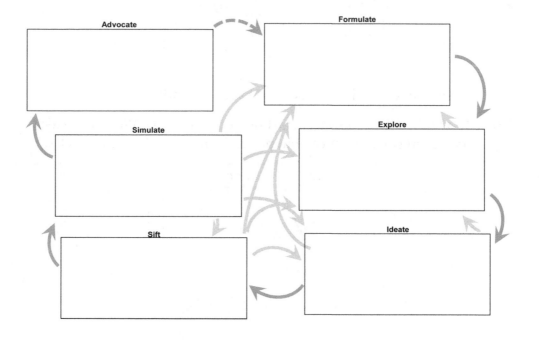

Appendix J

The Design Process ThinkSheet

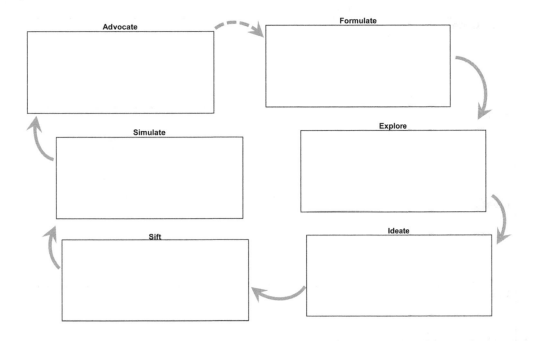

Advocate

Formulate

Simulate

Explore

Sift

Ideate

Appendix K
IDE Corp's Design Process

Formulate

Explore

Ideate

Sift

Simulate

Advocate